Southern Living®

CASSEROLES
COOKBOOK
by Jean Wickstrom
Foods Editor

Library of Congress Catalog Number: 74-78765
ISBN: 0-8487-0357-X

Manufactured in the United States of America

Fourth Printing 1986

Cover Photo: Taylor Lewis

Cover Recipe: Chicken Salonika

Illustrations: Elinor Williams

CONTENTS

INTRODUCTION

Casserole cooking is more than just a happy use of leftovers and a glorified use of less expensive cuts of meat. The wonderful thing about casseroles is the convenience of combining a variety of foods that meld together into an appetizing and hearty dish.

Being so perfectly suited to our modern way of life, the casserole's many virtues are self-evident. Casseroles are a boon to the busy homemaker because most of them contain all the ingredients for a one-dish meal and can be prepared hours before serving or days ahead and frozen. Also, casseroles can go from oven to table in the attractive vessel they were cooked in.

There is practically no limit to the ingredients that can be included in casseroles, thus offering opportunity for variety and creativity in meal planning. Since casseroles can be prepared quickly, they are the cook's answer for what to serve on a busy day. Just add a salad and your meal is complete.

You'll find dishes suitable for any occasion in this vast assortment of over 300 casserole recipes. Besides being delicious, these selected recipes are time-savers as well as money-savers.

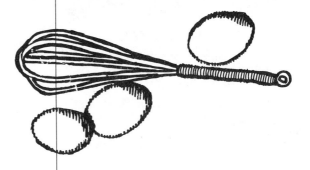

ALL ABOUT CASSEROLES

This book of casseroles offers delicious recipes featuring a variety of meats plus vegetable, egg, and cheese recipes for meatless days.

In addition to the recipes, information on the many types of casserole dishes, how seasonings transform a simple dish into gourmet fare, and preparation of casseroles for the freezer proves helpful.

TYPES OF CASSEROLE DISHES

The word "casserole" means more than a one-dish savory blend of meat, vegetables, and seasonings. It also means the cooking vessel in which these flavorful combinations are cooked.

Casserole dishes vary in shape, size, and materials. These baking dishes may be oblong, square, oval, or round and can vary in size from individual servings to crowd capacity. Many have handles and covers and easily go from oven to table. Some casserole dishes are almost as shallow as a platter, while others are high and straight-sided for soufflés. Gleaming electric casseroles with hidden heating controls are attractive enough to go straight to the table.

Today's classic cooking vessel is made from just about every material from earthenware used in French casseroles to freezer-to-oven glassware and pyroceram so popular with the American homemaker. Simple earthenware dishes made of terra cotta are porous and glazed on the inside and top. Beautiful casserole dishes are also available in California clay. These flameproof casseroles are made of thick pottery glazed on the inside and cover; some are also glazed on the outside. Ovenproof clear glass casseroles can be dressed up when set in a gaily decorated basket or metal holder. Because enameled casseroles are sturdy, decorative, and keep food warm, they are very popular. Enameled casseroles are cast iron, aluminum, or stainless steel with a baked porcelain enamel coating.

All casserole dishes should be thoroughly cleaned after each use; stains allowed to accumulate are hard to remove. Most containers can be washed in warm soapy water. Stubborn stains can be removed from glass, enamel, aluminum, and steel by scouring with cleaning pads or a fine cleansing powder.

With today's unlimited variety in casserole dishes, select casseroles that suit the occasion or food. All casseroles, from the most decorative to the simplest earthen one, are meant to come right to the table.

SEASONINGS

Seasonings can make casseroles something special by bringing out the full, natural flavor of every ingredient. Herbs and spices work two ways: they enhance the natural flavor of foods and add an interesting new flavor to a rather bland food. Herbs are the leaves of Temperate Zone plants; spices are made from the root, flower, seed, or bark of pungent plants grown in the Tropics.

Use a light hand when experimenting with new seasonings. Since the pungency of each herb and spice differs and its effect on foods varies, there is no set rule for the amount to use. Tips to remember in experimenting with seasonings: (1) ground spices are more pungent than whole spices, (2) heat increases the pungency of spices, and (3) dried herbs are more pungent than fresh herbs, so use less (about 1/4 the amount).

Most seasonings can be purchased in whole form, ground, or powdered. Whole seasonings need more time to impart flavoring to food, but can be removed at any point in cooking. It is a good idea to put them in a small cheesecloth bag or in an aluminum teaball for convenience in removing. Whole seasonings are especially useful in long-cooking dishes. Ground and powdered seasonings impart flavor quickly. When used in a medium to long cooking dish, they should be added near the end of the cooking time.

Seasonings should be stored in a cool, dry place since heat robs their flavor and dampness cakes them. Protect the volatile oils by keeping the containers tightly closed. Seasonings that stand on the shelf too long lose their flavor; therefore, it may be wise to buy small containers and replace them frequently.

Use herbs and spices sparingly or just enough to heighten natural food flavors. Seasonings can turn the simplest dish into an epicurean delight.

PREPARING CASSEROLES FOR THE FREEZER

The greatest virtue of casserole cookery is its prepare-ahead feature. Most casseroles are ideal for advance preparation and even suitable for freezer storage.

Since various foods react differently to freezing, it is wise to know how well ingredients in the casserole will freeze. The flavor or texture of the following foods frequently changes during the freezing process:

(1) Crumb or cheese toppings are best added when the food is reheated for serving. Some cheese toppings can be added the last 15 minutes of cooking time.

(2) Raw vegetables often lose their crispness in casseroles that are frozen.

(3) Green pepper, garlic, and clove become stronger in flavor after freezing, while onions, most herb seasonings, and salt lose flavor.

(4) Noodles, spaghetti, and macaroni have a better flavor if added to the casserole during the thawing process.

(5) Hard-cooked egg whites become tough when they are frozen unless they are sieved. Hard-cooked egg yolks should be sieved or diced before freezing.

(6) Sauces and mayonnaise often separate during freezing, but the original consistency is often restored by stirring during the thawing process. Do not substitute salad dressing for mayonnaise in freezer dishes because separation is more apt to occur.

(7) Potatoes, particularly those diced, become mushy when thawed.

It is often a good idea to shorten the cooking time of a casserole to be frozen since the casserole will be reheated before serving. If the casserole is to be frozen, remove it from the range and chill as rapidly as possible. This stops the cooking and retards or prevents the growth of bacteria that may cause spoilage.

Many dishes can be frozen in the casserole they were baked in and then reheated in the same dish, or the casserole can be lined with heavy-duty aluminum foil and the food frozen in it. When the casserole is solidly frozen, lift out the package, wrap, seal securely with freezer tape, and return to the freezer.

All freezer packages should be labeled with the name of the casserole and the date of freezing. Since most frozen dishes require thawing or heating before serving, label and include specific instructions on the freezer package.

The freezing process should be completed as rapidly as possible. Most casseroles can be safely frozen for three to four months or longer, depending on the ingredients used.

A quick method of thawing casseroles is to heat the frozen dish in the oven at the original cooking temperature. This method works well with most casseroles except very large ones where the heat may not penetrate to thaw and warm the center. If a casserole is to be thawed completely before reheating, it is usually best to thaw in the refrigerator. Due to possible spoilage, thawing at room temperature is not recommended. Many of today's wide variety of handsome baking dishes go directly from the freezer, into the hot oven, and straight to the table.

BEEF CASSEROLES

BEEF AND CABBAGE

> 4 slices bacon, finely diced
> 1 large onion, finely diced
> 1 teaspoon salt
> Pepper to taste
> 1 teaspoon poultry seasoning
> 1 egg, slightly beaten
> 1/2 cup soft breadcrumbs
> 2 pounds lean ground beef
> 1 head cabbage, shredded
> 1 (10-1/2-ounce) can beef bouillon

Fry bacon until crisp; add onion and sauté until onion is transparent but not brown. Add salt, pepper, poultry seasoning, egg, and breadcrumbs to beef. Mix with onion and bacon. Place a layer of shredded cabbage in a 3-quart casserole dish; top with a layer of the meat mixture. Continue alternating layers, ending with cabbage. Pour bouillon over all. Cover and bake at 350° for 1-1/2 hours. Remove cover during the last 15 minutes to brown cabbage. Yield: 6 servings.

BEEF AND RICE BAKE

> 2 tablespoons salad oil or shortening
> 1 medium onion, chopped
> 1 green pepper, cut into thin rings
> 1 clove garlic, minced
> 1 pound ground beef
> 1 cup cooked rice, salted
> Salt to taste
> Dash pepper
> 1 (16-ounce) can tomatoes

Put oil in a skillet, heat, and add the chopped onion, green pepper, and garlic. When this has lightly browned, add ground beef, stirring until lightly brown. Place in a casserole dish. Add cooked rice, salt, pepper, and tomatoes; mix well. A small amount of water may be added to mixture. Cool and freeze. To serve, thaw overnight in refrigerator and bake at 300° for about 45 minutes. Yield: 6 servings.

BEEF AND SQUASH CASSEROLE

> 4 cups cooked yellow crookneck squash
> 1 pound lean ground beef
> 1/2 cup chopped onion
> 1 tablespoon butter or margarine
> 2 cups cooked rice
> 1 teaspoon salt
> 1 (10-3/4-ounce) can cream of
>   mushroom soup
> 2 cups buttered breadcrumbs

Drain cooked squash. Brown ground beef and onion in butter and add to cooked rice. Season with salt. Place half of the squash into a 2- to 2-1/2-quart baking dish. Cover squash with beef mixture. Add a second layer of squash. Cover with mushroom soup and sprinkle with breadcrumbs. Bake at 350° for 35 to 40 minutes. Yield: 8 servings.

BEEF-BACON CASSEROLE

> 12 slices bacon, diced
> 2 pounds lean ground beef
> 1 medium onion, chopped
> 2 (5-ounce) packages narrow noodles,
>   cooked and drained
> 2 (10-3/4-ounce) cans tomato soup
> 2 (10-3/4-ounce) cans cream of
>   mushroom soup
> 1 (1-pound) can peas, drained
> Salt and pepper to taste
> 1 cup buttered breadcrumbs
> 1 to 1-1/2 cups shredded sharp Cheddar
>   cheese

Fry bacon, ground beef, and onion together until lightly browned; drain off all excess fat. Add noodles, soups, and peas; mix well. Add salt and pepper to taste, if needed. Place mixture into two 3-1/2-quart casserole dishes; seal and freeze. To serve, thaw and top with buttered breadcrumbs and shredded cheese; bake at 325° for 45 minutes. Yield: 12 to 15 servings.

BEEF-BISCUIT PIE

1-1/2 teaspoons salt, divided
1/8 teaspoon pepper
3 tablespoons all-purpose flour
1-1/2 pounds beef stew meat, cut into
1-1/2-inch cubes
3 tablespoons shortening
3-1/2 cups water
2 celery stalks with leaves, finely chopped
1 bay leaf
6 whole cloves
12 small white onions
6 medium carrots, sliced
3 medium potatoes, peeled and cut in halves

Blend together 1/2 teaspoon of the salt, the pepper, and flour, and toss lightly over meat to coat. Reserve leftover flour. Put shortening in a heavy skillet; add beef and brown. Add water, 1/2 teaspoon of the salt, celery, bay leaf, and cloves. Cover; simmer for 2 to 2-1/2 hours, or until meat is almost tender. Add remaining salt and vegetables. Cover, and cook until vegetables are tender. Measure reserved flour; add enough to make 2 tablespoons. Add 3 tablespoons water; stir to a smooth paste. Gradually add to stew, stirring until thickened. Place in a 3-quart casserole dish and arrange biscuits around edge. Bake at 425° for 10 to 15 minutes, or until biscuits are well done. Yield: 6 to 8 servings.

BEEF-CABBAGE CASSEROLE

1 medium head cabbage (about 3 pounds)
1 cup uncooked regular rice
1 pound ground chuck
1 teaspoon salt
1/2 teaspoon pepper
1 small onion, chopped (optional)
1 (8-ounce) can tomato sauce
Water

Cut cabbage into quarters, remove core, and drop into boiling water. Cook for about 5 minutes or until cabbage is tender. Cook rice according to package directions. Mix rice, ground chuck, salt, and pepper in a large bowl. Add onion, if desired.

Remove cabbage from water and drain. Make a layer of cabbage leaves in bottom of a heavily oiled 3-quart casserole dish; add a layer of rice and beef mixture. Repeat layers, with a layer of cabbage leaves on top. Spread tomato sauce over top and add enough water to keep mixture from sticking. You may need to add additional water as mixture cooks. Bake at 350° for about 1 hour. Yield: 8 to 10 servings.

BEEF-BEAN CASSEROLE

1-1/2 pounds lean ground beef
1 small onion, minced
1/2 cup catsup
1/2 teaspoon dry mustard
2 tablespoons vinegar
3 tablespoons dark brown sugar
1 (17-ounce) can green lima beans
1 (15-ounce) can red kidney beans
1 (21-ounce) can pork and beans
1/2 teaspoon salt

Brown beef in a heavy skillet; add onion and cook until transparent but not brown. Add other ingredients; mix well. Place mixture into two 1-1/2-quart casserole dishes. Seal well; freeze, or bake at once at 350° for 30 minutes. Yield: 10 servings.

MEATBALL CASSEROLE

1-1/2 pounds ground beef
3/4 cup uncooked regular oats
1 cup evaporated milk
1 tablespoon dehydrated onion flakes
1 teaspoon salt
1/2 teaspoon pepper
1 cup catsup
2 tablespoons vinegar
1/2 cup water
2 tablespoons sugar

Combine meat, oats, milk, onion flakes, salt, and pepper. Mix well; shape into 8 large meatballs, and place in a 2-quart casserole dish. Combine catsup, vinegar, water, and sugar; and pour over top of the meatballs. Bake at 350° for 1-1/2 hours. Yield: 8 servings.

BEEF EN CASSEROLE

    2 pounds beef chuck, cut into 1-1/2-inch
      cubes
    3 tablespoons all-purpose flour
    3 tablespoons shortening
  1/2 teaspoon pepper
    1 teaspoon salt
  1/2 teaspoon thyme
    2 teaspoons parsley flakes
    1 bay leaf
    1 cup beef bouillon
    1 (6-ounce) can tomato paste
  1/2 cup red cooking wine
    6 small white onions, peeled and left whole
    6 medium carrots, scraped and quartered
    1 cup sliced celery

Using a heavy pan, brown floured meat
slowly in hot shortening. Place meat in a 3-quart
casserole dish. Mix pepper, salt, thyme, and
parsley flakes, and sprinkle over meat. Add bay
leaf. Combine beef bouillon, tomato paste, and
wine and pour over meat. Cover the casserole
and bake at 325° for 1-1/2 hours. Add
vegetables, cover, and bake an additional 40
minutes. Yield: 6 servings.

BURGUNDY BEEF

    2 pounds cubed lean beef
  1/4 cup all-purpose flour
    1 tablespoon salt
  1/4 teaspoon pepper
  1/4 cup bacon drippings
    1 cup water
    1 cup Burgundy
    6 carrots
    6 small onions
    1 (10-ounce) package frozen peas
    6 medium potatoes, cooked, seasoned,
      and mashed
    1 egg yolk, beaten
    1 tablespoon cream

Dredge cubes of beef in flour seasoned with
salt and pepper. Brown meat in bacon drippings;
add water and wine. Cover and simmer for
45 minutes. Pare carrots and peel onions; add to
meat and cook 45 minutes longer, or until
vegetables are tender.
Cook peas according to package directions
and set aside. Cook potatoes; mash and season
as desired. Add peas to meat mixture and put
in a 3-quart casserole dish; flute potatoes around
the edges of the dish. Brush with mixture of egg
yolk and cream; cool and freeze. To serve, thaw

and bake at 350° for 15 to 20 minutes, or until
potatoes are lightly browned. Yield: 6 servings.
Variation: This casserole can be frozen
without the mashed potatoes, which can be
added (fluted and brushed) after the casserole
has been partially heated.

CASSEROLE INTERNATIONAL

    3 cups cooked prime rib roast, cut into
      large cubes
    1 cup tomato juice
    2 small cloves garlic, minced
  1/2 teaspoon fines herbs
    1 teaspoon curry powder
    1 teaspoon minced green pepper
    1 (10-ounce) package frozen chow mein
    1 cup cooked fettucine (macaroni)
  1/2 cup cooking sherry
  1/2 cup shredded sharp Cheddar cheese
    2 tablespoons minced parsley

Simmer cooked roast beef for 15 minutes in
tomato juice with minced garlic, herbs, curry
powder, and green pepper. Add frozen chow
mein and simmer until it is thawed and blended
with other ingredients. Add the cooked fettucine
and cooking sherry, stirring all ingredients
to distribute evenly. If more moisture is required,
add tomato juice. Place in a greased casserole
dish and sprinkle top with cheese and parsley.
Bake at 300° for 15 minutes. Yield: 4 to 6
servings.

CHEESEBURGER PIE

    1 pound ground beef
  1/2 cup evaporated milk
  1/2 cup catsup
  1/3 cup fine dry breadcrumbs
  1/4 cup chopped onion
  1/2 teaspoon crushed oregano
  3/4 teaspoon salt
  1/8 teaspoon pepper
    1 (9-inch) unbaked pie shell
    4 ounces American cheese, shredded
    1 teaspoon Worcestershire sauce

Combine ground beef, milk, catsup,
breadcrumbs, onion, oregano, salt, and pepper in
a large bowl. Mix well with hands. Pat mixture
into the unbaked pie shell. Bake at 350° for
35 to 40 minutes. Toss cheese with
Worcestershire sauce and sprinkle on top of
pie; bake 10 minutes longer. Let sit for about 10
minutes, cut into wedges to serve. Yield:
6 servings.

CHEESE-STUFFED MANICOTTI WITH MEAT SAUCE

1/2 pound ground beef
1/3 cup chopped green pepper
1 large clove garlic, minced
1 teaspoon Italian seasoning, crushed
2 (10-3/4-ounce) cans tomato soup
1/2 cup water
4 cups (2 pounds) creamed small curd cottage cheese
2 eggs, slightly beaten
1/2 cup grated Parmesan cheese
1/2 cup chopped parsley
1 (5- to 8-ounce) package manicotti macaroni, cooked
3 slices (3 ounces) Mozzarella, cut in half

Brown meat and cook green pepper, garlic, and Italian seasoning until green pepper is tender. Stir in soup and water. Meanwhile, combine cottage cheese, eggs, Parmesan cheese, and parsley; use to fill cooked manicotti macaroni. Arrange manicotti in a shallow baking dish; cover with sauce. Bake at 350° for 45 minutes. Top with Mozzarella cheese. Bake until cheese melts. Yield: 4 to 6 servings.

COMPANY BEEF CASSEROLE

1 pound ground beef
2 tablespoons shortening
1 medium onion, chopped
2 cups canned tomatoes
1 tablespoon catsup
1 tablespoon steak sauce
1/4 cup chopped green pepper
2 tablespoons chopped parsley
1 (5-ounce) package elbow macaroni
Salt and pepper to taste
1 (10-3/4-ounce) can cream of mushroom soup
1 cup shredded Cheddar cheese

Brown ground beef in shortening in heavy skillet until gray. Add onion, tomatoes, catsup, steak sauce, green pepper, and parsley. Simmer for 30 minutes. Cook macaroni according to package directions. Combine macaroni and ground beef mixture in a 2-quart baking dish. Season to taste. Gently spoon mushroom soup into mixture. Mix lightly, lifting from the bottom. Sprinkle shredded cheese over the top. Bake at 350° for 30 minutes, or until top is bubbly and browned. Yield: 6 servings.

BEEF-MACARONI CASSEROLE

2 medium onions, sliced
4 tablespoons butter or margarine
1 pound ground beef
1 teaspoon salt
Dash pepper
1/2 teaspoon cumin
1/2 teaspoon oregano
1/8 teaspoon curry powder
1 (10-ounce) package macaroni, cooked and drained
1 cup shredded American cheese
1/4 cup crumbled blue cheese (optional)
1 (10-3/4-ounce) can tomato soup
1 cup milk
Buttered breadcrumbs

Sauté onions in butter until soft. Add meat, salt, pepper, cumin, oregano, and curry powder; brown lightly.

In a buttered 1-1/2-quart casserole dish, add a layer of cooked macaroni, top with a layer of meat mixture, then a layer of shredded and crumbled cheese. Repeat layers. Mix soup and milk and pour over mixture. Top with buttered breadcrumbs and bake at 375° for 30 minutes. Yield: 6 to 8 servings.

BEEF-ZUCCHINI CASSEROLE

1-1/2 pounds zucchini squash
1 pound lean ground beef
1/2 cup chopped onion
1 teaspoon seasoned salt or garlic salt
1 teaspoon oregano
2 cups cooked rice
1 (16-ounce) carton small curd creamed cottage cheese
1 (10-3/4-ounce) can cream of mushroom soup, undiluted
Buttered breadcrumbs or cracker crumbs

Cut or slice squash (do not peel) into 1-inch pieces and cook in boiling salted water until barely tender. Drain well. Brown beef and onion; drain off excess fat. Add seasonings and cooked rice to beef mixture. Place half of the squash in a 3-quart casserole dish; spread beef mixture over squash. Cover with cottage cheese, then with the rest of the squash. Spread mushroom soup over all. Sprinkle crumbs over the top. Bake at 350° for 35 to 40 minutes. Yield: 6 to 8 servings.

EGGPLANT-MEAT CASSEROLE

1 pound ground beef
  Salt and pepper to taste
2 tablespoons salad oil
1 medium eggplant
1/3 cup all-purpose flour
1/4 cup olive oil
2 (8-ounce) cans tomato sauce
1/2 teaspoon oregano
1 tablespoon grated Parmesan cheese
1 cup shredded Cheddar cheese

Shape ground beef into patties; season to taste with salt and pepper. Brown in hot oil. Slice unpeeled eggplant into thick slices. Season with salt and pepper, coat with flour, and brown in olive oil. Place cooked eggplant slices into a shallow baking dish. Top each slice with a browned meat patty. Cover with tomato sauce. Sprinkle oregano and Parmesan cheese over all. Top with shredded Cheddar cheese. Bake at 300° for 35 minutes. Yield: 6 servings.

ENCHILADA CASSEROLE

2 pounds lean ground beef
3 small onions, chopped
  Dash garlic powder
1 (4-ounce) can green chiles, chopped
1 dozen tortillas
1 (10-ounce) can enchilada sauce
1/2 pound shredded Cheddar cheese
1 (10-3/4-ounce) can cream of mushroom soup

Combine ground beef, onions, garlic powder, and green chiles in a skillet. Simmer for about 20 minutes, stirring occasionally.

Dip 3 tortillas in enchilada sauce and place in the bottom of a greased flat casserole dish. Add 1/4 of the meat mixture, spreading to form a thin layer. Add 1/4 of the shredded cheese, then 1/4 of the soup. Continue layers of tortillas, meat, cheese, and soup until all ingredients have been used. Pour any remaining enchilada sauce over the top. Bake at 450° for 20 minutes. Yield: 8 servings.

CHILI CON CARNE CASSEROLE

1 pound ground beef
1 tablespoon shortening
1 (1-pound) can kidney beans, undrained
1 (10-3/4-ounce) can tomato soup, undiluted
1 teaspoon salt
2 teaspoons chili powder
1/4 cup instant minced onions

Brown meat in shortening. Add kidney beans, undiluted tomato soup, salt, chili powder, and instant minced onion. Mix well. Spoon into a 1-quart casserole dish. Bake at 350° for 40 minutes. Serve hot as main dish. Yield: 6 servings.

FAVORITE CASSEROLE

12 slices bacon, diced
2 pounds ground beef
1 medium onion, chopped
2 (5-ounce) packages noodles, cooked and drained
2 (10-3/4-ounce) cans tomato soup, undiluted
2 (10-3/4-ounce) cans cream of mushroom soup, undiluted
1 (1-pound) can English peas, drained
1 cup buttered cracker crumbs
1-1/2 cups shredded sharp Cheddar cheese

Fry bacon, ground beef, and onion together until lightly browned. Pour off all excess fat. Mix noodles with ground beef mixture, soups, and peas. Place into two 3-1/2-quart casserole dishes. Top with cracker crumbs, and add cheese for topping. Bake at 300° to 325° for 45 minutes. One casserole may be frozen for later use. Yield: 10 to 12 servings.

GERMAN MEAT CASSEROLE

3 large potatoes, thinly sliced
5 carrots, quartered
1 small onion, diced
2 tablespoons butter or margarine, melted
1 pound lean ground beef
1 tablespoon catsup
1 (10-3/4-ounce) can cream of mushroom soup
1 (4-ounce) can button mushrooms, drained
2 tablespoons butter or margarine, melted
1 (3-1/2-ounce) can French fried onion rings

Parboil potatoes and carrots for 20 minutes. Sauté onion in 2 tablespoons butter, add beef and cook until it turns gray. Butter a 2-1/2-quart casserole dish. Alternate layers of beef and onion mixture and vegetables. Mix catsup with soup and pour over the casserole. Sauté mushrooms in 2 tablespoons butter and place on top of the casserole. Sprinkle onion rings over mushrooms. Bake at 350° for about 20 minutes, or until onion rings are brown and crisp. Yield: 6 servings.

HAMBURGER STROGANOFF

    1 (6-ounce) package egg noodles
1/2 cup chopped onion
1/4 cup butter or margarine, melted
    1 pound ground beef
    1 tablespoon all-purpose flour
1/2 teaspoon garlic salt
    1 (8-ounce) can tomato sauce with
      mushrooms
1/4 cup Burgundy
    1 (10-1/2-ounce) can beef bouillon
    1 teaspoon salt
1/4 teaspoon pepper
    1 cup commercial sour cream
1/2 cup grated Parmesan cheese

Cook noodles according to package directions; drain and set aside. Sauté onion in butter; add beef and stir until brown and crumbly. Pour off excess fat. Add flour and stir well. Add garlic salt, tomato sauce, wine, bouillon, salt, and pepper. Blend well and simmer for 10 minutes. Stir in sour cream, and remove from heat.

Alternate layers of cooked noodles and meat sauce in a greased 2-quart casserole dish, ending with sauce. Sprinkle Parmesan cheese on top. Bake at 375° for 25 to 30 minutes, or until bubbly. Casserole freezes well. Yield: 6 servings.

HUNGARIAN BEEF-RICE CASSEROLE

    1 pound beef stew meat
      Bacon drippings
    1 teaspoon basil
    1 teaspoon paprika
    1 teaspoon pepper
    1 tablespoon salt
    1 (11-ounce) can tomato-rice soup
1/2 soup can warm water
    1 tablespoon Worcestershire sauce
    1 (1-pound) jar small onions, drained
    2 to 3 medium potatoes, sliced
    1 bay leaf
      Cooked rice

Brown beef in bacon drippings. Pour off fat and season meat with basil, paprika, pepper, and salt. Mix soup, water, and Worcestershire sauce in a 2-quart casserole dish. Add drained onions, sliced potatoes, bay leaf, and beef; mix well. Cover casserole dish and bake at 325° for about 2 hours, or until tomato sauce has thickened and potatoes are done. Serve over fluffy rice. Yield: 4 servings.

COOL CASSEROLE

    2 pounds ground meat
    1 large onion, finely chopped
    1 large green pepper, diced
    3 (15-ounce) cans spaghetti with
      tomato sauce
    1 (4-ounce) can mushrooms,
      including liquid
    1 (8-ounce) can tomatoes, including juice
      Oregano (optional)

Brown the ground meat with the onion and green pepper. Add the remaining ingredients. Place into a 2-quart casserole dish and bake at 350° for 30 minutes. Cool and freeze, or you may freeze before baking; then remove from the freezer, allowing enough time for it to thaw before baking. If baked first, it will have to be thawed and then warmed in the oven for serving. This improves with age. Sprinkle with oregano before serving, if desired. Yield: 6 to 8 servings.

DO-AHEAD BEEF-MACARONI DINNER

1-1/2 cups macaroni
    2 teaspoons shortening
1/2 cup chopped onion
    1 pound ground beef
    1 teaspoon salt
    1 teaspoon steak sauce
1/4 teaspoon pepper
1/2 cup catsup
1-1/2 cups shredded cheese
    1 egg
1-1/2 cups milk
1/2 cup catsup

Cook macaroni according to package directions. Drain, and place in a large mixing bowl. Place shortening in a skillet and cook the chopped onion until browned. Add ground beef and cook until meat is gray. Pour off excess fat. Add salt, steak sauce, pepper, and 1/2 cup catsup. Mix the meat and macaroni; let cool. When mixture is cool, add shredded cheese and mix well. Place mixture into two 1-quart casserole dishes.

To bake, mix together egg, milk, 1/2 cup catsup, and additional shredded cheese, if desired. Pour over the casserole mixture and bake, covered, at 350° for about 25 to 30 minutes, or until it heats through and starts to bubble. Yield: 8 servings.

Note: This is an excellent dish to make ahead of time and freeze.

BEEF-EGGPLANT CASSEROLE

    2 cups ground beef
    1 tablespoon butter or margarine, melted
    2 cups cooked, mashed eggplant
    2 cups cooked rice
    1 (10-3/4-ounce) can cream of
      mushroom soup
    Salt and pepper to taste
1/2 cup crushed salty crackers

Sauté ground beef in butter until it is gray. Add other ingredients except cracker crumbs. Put into a buttered casserole dish and top with cracker crumbs. Bake at 350° for 25 to 30 minutes. Serve hot. Yield: 4 to 6 servings.

ITALIAN LASAGNA

1/2 cup chopped onion
    1 clove garlic, minced
    2 tablespoons butter or margarine, melted
    1 pound ground beef
    1 (1-pound) can tomatoes, sieved
    1 (6-ounce) can tomato paste
    1 (8-ounce) can tomato sauce
1-1/2 cups water
    1 teaspoon salt
1/2 teaspoon pepper
    1 teaspoon basil
    1 teaspoon oregano
1/4 teaspoon chili powder
    1 bay leaf
    1 teaspoon parsley flakes
    1 (10-ounce) package lasagna noodles
    2 eggs
    3 cups ricotta or cottage cheese
    1 cup grated Parmesan cheese
    1 pound Mozzarella cheese ,thinly sliced

Sauté onion and garlic in melted butter. Add beef and stir until brown. Add tomatoes, tomato paste, tomato sauce, water, salt, pepper, basil, oregano, chili powder, bay leaf, and parsley flakes. Simmer, covered, over low heat for 1-1/2 hours. Stir occasionally.

About 30 minutes before sauce is done, cook the lasagna noodles according to package directions. Drain.

Beat eggs and combine with ricotta cheese.

In a 13- x 9- x 2-inch casserole dish, alternate layers of lasagna noodles, sauce, egg and cheese mixture, grated Parmesan cheese, and sliced Mozzarella cheese. Repeat layers 3 times, ending with Mozzarella cheese. Bake at 375° for 30 minutes. Let stand for 15 minutes before serving. Yield: 8 to 10 servings.

ITALIAN MEAT CASSEROLE

    1 pound ground beef
1/2 cup chopped onion
    1 clove garlic, minced
1/2 to 1 teaspoon oregano
1/2 teaspoon salt
    1 (10-3/4-ounce) can tomato soup
1/3 cup water
    1 (5-ounce) package noodles, cooked and
      drained
    1 cup shredded Cheddar cheese

Brown beef in a skillet with onion, garlic, oregano, and salt. Combine meat mixture in a 1-1/2-quart casserole dish with soup, water, and cooked noodles. Sprinkle cheese over top, and bake at 350° for 30 minutes, or until cheese is melted. Yield: 4 to 5 servings.

JOHNNY MARZETTI

    6 medium onions, chopped
1-1/2 pounds ground chuck
1-1/2 teaspoons salt
1/4 teaspoon garlic salt
1/8 teaspoon pepper
1/4 cup butter or margarine, melted
    1 (16-ounce) package shell macaroni
1/4 cup butter or margarine
    4 cups shredded sharp Cheddar cheese,
      divided
    2 (8-ounce) cans tomato sauce
    2 (3-ounce) cans mushroom pieces
1/4 cup Burgundy

Sauté onions, ground chuck, salt, garlic salt, and pepper in 1/4 cup butter for about 15 minutes, stirring often with fork to prevent meat mixture from sticking.

Cook macaroni according to package directions, and drain. Toss macaroni with 1/4 cup butter and place into two 2-quart casserole dishes. Add 2-1/2 cups cheese to meat mixture, and stir until cheese melts. Add 1 can tomato sauce and the mushrooms; mix well. Pour mixture over macaroni, and top with the other can of tomato sauce and remaining cheese. Cool quickly. Wrap for freezing, or bake at 325° for 1 hour and 40 minutes. Pour wine on top before serving. Yield: 8 servings.

Note: If casserole is frozen, the day before serving, remove casserole from the freezer and thaw in the refrigerator. Bake according to previous directions.

CASSOULET

2 pounds dried white beans
1 bay leaf
1 stalk celery, chopped
1 tablespoon salt
1 teaspoon pepper
1 medium onion, stuck with 3 whole cloves
1 ham shank, preferably with meat on it
Few sprigs fresh parsley

Soak beans overnight in a large kettle in water to cover (or cover with water, bring to a boil, simmer 2 minutes, remove from heat, and let stand 1 hour). Add all other ingredients and more water if needed to cover the beans about 1/2 inch. Partially cover and simmer slowly until beans are almost, but not quite, done.

While beans cook, prepare the following:

4 slices bacon, diced
4 medium onions, chopped
5 cloves garlic, minced
4 to 5 pounds lean beef, cut into 1-inch cubes
1/2 teaspoon rosemary
Salt, black pepper, and cayenne pepper to taste
1 cup dry red wine
1-1/2 pounds smoked link sausage (the fully cooked kind)

Fry bacon slowly until crisp; remove to paper towels to drain. Sauté onions and garlic in fat remaining in skillet until tender but not brown. Remove with slotted spoon; place in a large casserole dish. Brown meat cubes well on all sides (if necessary add a small amount of fat to skillet). Place browned meat in the casserole dish. Add seasonings and wine; stir in bacon. Cover tightly and bake at 300° for 2 to 3 hours, or until meat is tender. Do not allow to dry out; add more wine or broth if required. When meat is tender, add beans with liquid and sausage links cut into 1/2-inch slices. Cover and bake for 1 hour. Freezes well. Yield: 15 servings.

SPANISH CASSEROLE

1 large onion, chopped
1 large green pepper, chopped
Shortening
1 pound ground beef
2 cups corn
1 (10-3/4-ounce) can tomato soup
2 (3-ounce) cans mushroom slices
1 teaspoon chili powder
1 (5-ounce) package noodles
1/2 cup shredded cheese

Sauté onion and green pepper in a small amount of shortening. Add ground beef and brown. Then add corn, soup, mushrooms, and chili powder. Cook the noodles for 5 minutes. Drain and add to the meat mixture. Place in a 2-quart baking dish; sprinkle with cheese and bake at 350° for 30 minutes. Yield: 8 servings.

CHILLIGHETTI CASSEROLE

1 pound ground beef
1 large onion, chopped
2 tablespoons shortening
2 teaspoons chili powder
1 teaspoon salt
2 cups cooked red kidney beans
1-1/2 cups uncooked spaghetti
3 cups tomato juice
1 tablespoon Worcestershire sauce
2 teaspoons salt
1/2 teaspoon pepper

Brown ground beef and onion in shortening. Add chili powder and 1 teaspoon salt; simmer for about 5 minutes. Add beans and spaghetti; pour mixture in a 2-1/2-quart casserole dish. Combine remaining ingredients and pour over casserole. Cover and bake at 350° for 1 hour. Yield: 6 to 8 servings.

MEXICAN CASSEROLE

2 pounds ground chuck
1 cup chopped onion
1 (12-ounce) can whole kernel corn, drained
1 (10-3/4-ounce) can cream of celery soup, undiluted
1 (10-3/4-ounce) can cream of mushroom soup, undiluted
1 cup commercial sour cream
Hot pepper sauce to taste
Salt and pepper to taste
1 cup taco-flavored corn chips, divided
3 cups cooked noodles

Brown meat and onion lightly. Add next 6 ingredients and half of the corn chips. Mix well. Stir in noodles. Pour into a 2-quart casserole dish. Top with remaining corn chips. Cool in refrigerator; then freeze. When ready to serve, thaw overnight in the refrigerator and bake at 350° for 45 minutes. Yield: 6 servings.

ZESTY MEXICAN PIE

 1 pound ground lean steak
 1 tablespoon salad oil
 1 (1-3/4-ounce) envelope chili mix
1/2 cup water
 1 (1-pound) can tomatoes
 1 (1-pound) can kidney beans
 1 (8-ounce) can refrigerated biscuits
  Melted butter or margarine
1/2 cup chopped walnuts or peanuts

Brown beef in salad oil. Add chili mix, water, tomatoes, and beans and place in a shallow 3-quart baking dish. Bake at 450° for 15 minutes, stirring once. Put biscuits on top of meat mixture; brush tops with melted butter and sprinkle top with chopped nuts. Bake according to directions on biscuit package. Yield: 4 servings.

QUICK CHEESE STEAKS

 2 tablespoons grated onion
 1 tablespoon shortening
 4 cubed beef steaks
 1 (10-3/4-ounce) can tomato soup
 1 teaspoon sugar
1/4 teaspoon basil
 1 teaspoon salt
1/4 cup grated Parmesan cheese

Cook onion in melted shortening; add steaks and cook until brown. Add other ingredients except cheese. Put into a 1-1/2-quart casserole dish and cover tightly. Let cool; then seal and freeze. To bake, remove from freezer, thaw, and bake at 350° for 1 hour, or until steaks are tender. Sprinkle with cheese before serving. Yield: 4 servings.

RANCH CASSEROLE

1-1/2 pounds ground beef
 2 tablespoons shortening
 1 teaspoon salt
 1 (1-3/8-ounce) package dry onion
  soup mix
1/2 cup water
 1 cup catsup
 2 tablespoons prepared mustard
 2 tablespoons vinegar
1/2 cup piccalilli relish
  Cooked rice or buns

Sauté meat in shortening. Add remaining ingredients and cook in a covered skillet for about 30 minutes, or bake in a covered casserole dish at 325° for 30 to 40 minutes. Serve over rice or on buns. Yield: 6 to 8 servings.

TAMALE-CHEESE PIE

Filling

1/2 cup chopped onion
 1 clove garlic, minced
 1 tablespoon butter or margarine
1/2 pound ground beef
 1 cup sliced mushrooms
 1 (16-ounce) can tomatoes
 1 (12-ounce) can whole kernel corn,
  drained
 1 (8-ounce) can tomato sauce
1/4 cup chopped green pepper
 1 tablespoon chili powder
1-1/2 teaspoons salt
 1 cup sliced pitted black olives
 1 cup (1/4 pound) shredded sharp
  Cheddar cheese

Crust

3/4 cup cornmeal
 3 cups cold milk, divided
 1 tablespoon butter or margarine
 1 teaspoon salt
 2 eggs, beaten
 1 cup (1/4 pound) shredded sharp Cheddar
  cheese

Sauté onion and garlic in butter. Add beef and mushrooms; cook and stir until beef turns gray. Add tomatoes, corn, tomato sauce, green pepper, chili powder, and salt. Cover and simmer for about 45 minutes. Add olives and simmer for another 15 minutes.

Prepare crust by mixing cornmeal and 1 cup cold milk. In a saucepan, combine remaining 2 cups milk, butter, and salt; heat to boiling. Gradually add cornmeal mixture, stirring constantly; cook until thickened. Cover and cook over very low heat for about 15 minutes. Stir in eggs and 1 cup cheese; continue stirring until cheese is melted.

Line bottom of a buttered shallow 2-quart casserole dish with the cornmeal mixture, reserving 1-1/2 cups for top of pie. Pour meat filling over cornmeal mixture. Drop spoonsful of remaining cornmeal mixture over meat filling. Sprinkle remaining cup of shredded cheese over all. Bake at 350° for 50 to 60 minutes, or until browned and bubbly around edges. Yield: 6 to 8 servings.

Garlic

Garlic is a pungent herb that must be used with a light touch. It brings an unusual flavor to a wide range of dishes. About 1/4 teaspoon garlic powder is equal to one small clove garlic.

MACARONI WITH MEAT SAUCE

    2 tablespoons salad oil
  1/4 cup chopped onion
    1 clove garlic, minced
    1 pound ground beef
    1 cup diced celery
  1/2 cup diced green pepper
1-1/2 teaspoons salt
  1/4 teaspoon celery salt
    1 (20-ounce) can tomatoes
      Few drops hot pepper sauce
    1 teaspoon Worcestershire sauce
    1 (3- or 4-ounce) can mushrooms
    1 (8-ounce) package elbow macaroni,
      cooked
      Grated Parmesan cheese

Heat oil in a 10-inch skillet. Add onion and garlic; cook until onion is tender, but not brown. Add meat; break into small pieces; cook and stir until lightly browned. Add next 7 ingredients and bring to a boil. Cover; simmer for 45 minutes. Add mushrooms and heat to boiling. Arrange macaroni on a platter. Pour sauce over macaroni. Sprinkle with cheese. Yield: 6 servings.

HUSBAND'S DELIGHT CASSEROLE

    1 (8-ounce) package cream cheese, softened
    2 cups commercial sour cream
    3 green onions, chopped
1-1/2 pounds ground chuck
    2 tablespoons butter or margarine, melted
    2 (8-ounce) cans tomato sauce
    1 teaspoon sugar
    1 teaspoon salt
      Dash pepper
      Dash Worcestershire sauce
    2 (5-ounce) packages noodles
  1/2 cup shredded cheese

In a bowl, mix cream cheese, sour cream, and onions. Brown the meat in butter; add tomato sauce, sugar, salt, pepper, and Worcestershire sauce. Cook noodles according to package directions. In a 2-quart casserole dish, alternate layers of noodles, beef mixture, and sour cream mixture. Top with the shredded cheese and bake at 350° until brown. Yield: 8 servings.

Bay Leaf

Bay leaf has a sharp flavor and pungent fragrance. A bay leaf is usually removed from the dish before serving. It gives a pleasant flavor to hearty meat casseroles.

BAKED BEEF AND RICE

1-1/2 pounds ground beef
    1 cup uncooked regular rice
    1 small onion, chopped
    2 tablespoons shortening
1-1/2 teaspoons salt
  1/2 teaspoon pepper
    1 teaspoon paprika
    1 (2-ounce) jar stuffed olives, sliced
    2 cups tomato juice
1-1/2 cups boiling water
  1/2 cup shredded Cheddar cheese

Brown ground beef, rice, and onion in shortening. Pour off fat. Add salt, pepper, and paprika. Add sliced olives, tomato juice, and boiling water. Place in a 1-1/2-quart baking dish. Cover tightly and bake at 300° for 1 hour. Uncover; sprinkle with cheese, and continue baking for about 10 minutes, or until cheese is melted. Yield: 6 servings.

BAKED BEEF-SPAGHETTI CASSEROLE

    1 pound ground round steak
    1 medium onion, minced
    1 green pepper, chopped
    3 stalks celery, chopped
    2 tablespoons butter or margarine
    1 (10-3/4-ounce) can tomato soup,
      undiluted
    2 (3- or 4-ounce) cans mushroom slices
      Salt and pepper to taste
    1 (8-ounce) package spaghetti, cooked
  1/2 pound shredded sharp Cheddar cheese
    1 (10-3/4-ounce) can tomato soup,
      undiluted
  1/4 cup sliced stuffed olives

Cook ground steak, onion, pepper, and celery in butter until meat turns gray. Add tomato soup, mushrooms, salt, and pepper. Alternate layers of cooked spaghetti, meat sauce, and shredded cheese in a 2-1/2-quart casserole dish; top with mushroom soup. Cover and bake at 325° for 45 minutes. Place sliced olives on top before serving. Yield: 6 to 8 servings.

ORIENT CASSEROLE

1-1/2 pounds ground chuck
   1 small onion, chopped
1/2 cup chopped celery
   1 (8-ounce) can water chestnuts,
     drained and chopped
   1 (4-ounce) can mushrooms,
     drained and chopped
2/3 cup uncooked regular rice
   1 teaspoon salt
   1 teaspoon pepper
1/3 cup soy sauce

Brown meat, onion, and celery together. Drain chestnuts and mushrooms, reserving liquid. Add chestnuts, mushrooms, rice, salt, pepper, and soy sauce to the meat. Add water to reserved liquid to make 2 cups and add to the meat mixture. Stir just to mix. Place in a casserole dish, cover, and bake at 350° for 1 hour. Yield: 6 to 8 servings.

ORIENTAL BEEF-SPAGHETTI CASSEROLE

   1 (5-ounce) package thin spaghetti
   1 tablespoon salad oil
1/2 pound ground beef
1/2 pound ground pork
1/3 cup chopped onion
   1 cup chopped celery
1/2 cup chopped green pepper
   1 (6-ounce) can tomato paste
   1 (7-ounce) bottle 7-Up
1/2 cup catsup or chili sauce
1/4 teaspoon thyme
   1 (4-ounce) can sliced mushrooms
   1 (1-pound) can chop suey vegetables,
     drained
1-1/2 teaspoons salt
3/4 cup grated Parmesan cheese

Cook spaghetti according to package directions; drain and set aside. Heat salad oil; add beef, pork, onion, celery, and green pepper; cook for 10 minutes over medium heat. Stir in tomato paste, 7-Up, catsup, and thyme. Add mushrooms, chop suey vegetables, and salt. Simmer for 10 minutes.

Alternate layers of cooked spaghetti, meat sauce, and Parmesan cheese in a 4-quart casserole dish, ending with sauce and cheese. Bake at 350° for 45 minutes. Yield: 10 servings.

Note: To freeze, cool thoroughly after layers have been placed in casserole dish. Cover tightly and seal. To serve, thaw, add additional 7-Up if needed, and bake at 350° for 45 minutes.

TALARENA

   1 pound ground beef
   1 medium onion, chopped
   1 medium green pepper, chopped
   1 tablespoon shortening
   1 (16-ounce) can tomatoes
1/2 teaspoon garlic salt
   1 teaspoon chili powder
   1 teaspoon salt
1/2 teaspoon pepper
   1 (17-ounce) can cream-style corn
   3 cups cooked regular, long-grain rice
     Shredded Cheddar cheese

Brown beef, onion, and green pepper in shortening. Add tomatoes, garlic salt, chili powder, salt, and pepper. Simmer for about 15 minutes, stirring occasionally. Add cooked, unseasoned corn and rice. Mix well and pour into a buttered 2- to 2-1/2-quart baking dish. Top with shredded cheese. Bake, covered, at 350° for 20 to 30 minutes. Yield: 8 servings.

TALLEYRAND

   1 pound lean ground beef
   1 medium onion, chopped
   1 medium green pepper,
     chopped (optional)
   2 tablespoons salad oil
   2 (6-ounce) cans tomato paste
   1 (17-ounce) can whole kernel corn
   1 (5-ounce) package narrow egg noodles,
     cooked
     Salt to taste
     Pinch thyme
     Pinch oregano
     Garlic salt to taste
3/4 cup shredded sharp cheese

Brown meat, onion, and pepper in salad oil. Add tomato paste, corn, cooked noodles, salt, thyme, oregano, and garlic salt. Mix well, and place in a 3-quart casserole dish, or divide into 2 casserole dishes. Cover and freeze.

To cook, top with shredded cheese and bake thawed casserole at 325° for about 30 minutes. Yield: 8 to 10 servings.

OVEN MEAL

- 2 cups diced or thinly sliced raw potatoes
- 2 cups chopped celery
- 2 cups (about 1-1/2 pounds) ground beef
- 1 cup finely chopped green peppers
- 1 teaspoon salt
- 1 teaspoon pepper
- 2 cups canned tomatoes
- 1 cup sliced onion

Place potatoes, celery, beef, and green peppers by layers in a 3-quart casserole dish. Sprinkle salt and pepper over each layer. Pour tomatoes over top, then add a layer of sliced onion. Cover casserole and bake at 375° for 1-1/2 hours. Yield: 6 servings.

PARTY CASSEROLE

- 1 (8-ounce) package noodles
- 1 to 1-1/2 pounds ground chuck
- 1 tablespoon butter or margarine, melted
- 2 (8-ounce) cans tomato sauce
- 1 cup large curd cottage cheese
- 1 (8-ounce) package cream cheese, softened
- 1 cup commercial sour cream
- 1/3 cup minced scallions or green onions
- 1 teaspoon minced green pepper
- 2 teaspoons melted butter or margarine

Cook noodles according to package directions. Sauté meat in 1 tablespoon melted butter until brown; add tomato sauce. Combine cottage cheese, cream cheese, sour cream, scallions, and green pepper in a bowl. Spread half the noodles in a 2-1/2-quart casserole dish and top with the cheese mixture. Add the remaining noodles and top with melted butter. Spread meat and tomato mixture on top. Chill. Bake at 375° for about 30 minutes. Uncover and bake for 15 minutes more. Yield: 6 to 8 servings.

TOMATO-BEEF CASSEROLE

- 1/2 pound ground beef
- 1 medium onion, chopped
- 1 (10-3/4-ounce) can tomato soup
- 1/2 soup can water
- 1 cup English peas
- 1 cup cooked rice
- 1/2 cup shredded cheese

In a skillet, brown the beef and onion, stirring to separate meat. Stir in soup, water, peas, and rice. Spoon into a 1-1/2-quart casserole dish and cover with shredded cheese. Bake at 375° for about 20 to 25 minutes. Yield: 4 servings.

ROUND STEAK CASSEROLE

- 1/4 cup all-purpose flour
- 2 pounds round steak, cut into serving-size pieces
  Salt and pepper to taste
- 2 medium or 1 large onion, sliced
- 2 carrots, cubed

Pound flour into meat; sprinkle with salt and pepper. Roll up and secure with toothpicks. Alternate layers of steak, onion slices, and carrots in a casserole dish. Repeat layers until all ingredients are used, ending with steak. Cover with boiling water. Cover casserole dish and bake at 325° for 3 hours. Add water as necessary. Remove cover and brown if needed. Yield: 4 servings.

Note: The amount of flour used may be varied according to the desired thickness of the gravy.

SIMPLY DELICIOUS SKILLET DINNER

- 1 tablespoon shortening
- 1/2 pound ground beef
- 1 medium onion, chopped
- 1 small clove garlic, minced
- 2 tablespoons minced parsley
- 1 (6-ounce) can tomato paste
- 2-1/4 cups water
- 1 teaspoon sugar
- 1 teaspoon salt
  Dash pepper
- 1 (5-ounce) package noodles
  Grated Parmesan cheese

Melt shortening in a heavy skillet; add ground beef, onion, garlic, and parsley. Brown lightly. Combine tomato paste with water, sugar, salt, and pepper, mixing until smooth. Add to meat mixture, mixing well. Cover, reduce heat, and simmer for 10 minutes. Add noodles, cover, and cook until noodles are tender, stirring occasionally. Serve with Parmesan cheese. Yield: 4 servings.

PORK CASSEROLES

HEAVENLY DELIGHT HOT DISH

  1 pound veal steak, cut into cubes
  1 pound pork steak, cut into cubes
  1 small onion, chopped
  3 tablespoons butter or margarine, melted
  1 teaspoon salt
3/4 pound American cheese, cut into cubes
  1 (12-ounce) can whole kernel corn
  1 (8-ounce) package uncooked noodles
  2 (10-1/2-ounce) cans chicken and
     rice soup
  1 cup water
  1 green pepper, chopped
  1 (4-ounce) jar pimientos, chopped
  1 (6-ounce) can mushrooms
  1 cup breadcrumbs, buttered and browned

Brown meat and onion in butter. Add salt
and the next 8 ingredients. Place in a 4-quart
casserole dish and top with buttered
breadcrumbs. Bake at 300° for 1 hour. Yield:
8 to 10 servings.

PORK AND CELERY PIE

    1 pound ground lean pork shoulder
1-1/4 teaspoons salt
     Dash pepper
    1 cup thinly sliced carrots
    1 cup diced potatoes
    1 tablespoon shortening
    1 (10-3/4-ounce) can cream of celery soup
  3/4 cup water
     Pastry for 4 individual pies

Combine meat, seasonings, carrots, and
potatoes. Cook in melted shortening in a heavy
skillet until lightly brown. Blend in soup and
water. Pour into 4 greased individual casserole
dishes. Top with piecrust. Bake at 400° for
about 30 minutes, or until piecrust is done.
Yield: 4 servings.

PORK CHOP-RICE CASSEROLE

  3 or 4 pork chops
  2 tablespoons shortening
  1 cup uncooked regular rice
  1 (16-ounce) can tomatoes
  1 onion, sliced
  1 (10-1/2-ounce) can beef consommé
    Salt and pepper
  1 teaspoon thyme

Brown pork chops in a small amount of
shortening. Place uncooked rice in the bottom of
a greased 1-1/2-quart casserole dish; lay cooked
pork chops on rice. Add the other ingredients
and cook at 350° for about 1 hour. Yield: 3 to 4
servings.

PORK CHOP AND APPLE CASSEROLE

  4 lean pork chops
    Salt
  1 tablespoon shortening
  4 cups sliced, tart cooking apples
1/4 cup raisins
  1 teaspoon grated lemon rind
1/4 cup molasses
1/4 cup water

Sprinkle pork chops with salt; sauté in
shortening until brown. Mix apples, raisins, and
lemon rind; place in a greased 2-quart baking
dish. Combine molasses and water and pour over
the apple mixture. Top with brown pork chops;
cover and bake at 350° for 1 hour. Remove cover
and bake an additional 30 minutes. Yield:
4 servings.

PORK AND MUSHROOM CASSEROLE

       3 slices bacon
     1/3 cup diced onion
     1/2 cup canned mushrooms, drained and
           liquid reserved
       1 pound pork tenderloin
       1 teaspoon salt
     1/8 teaspoon pepper
       1 egg, beaten
       1 cup fine breadcrumbs
     1/4 cup mushroom liquid

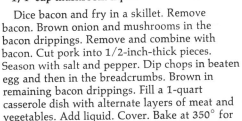

Dice bacon and fry in a skillet. Remove bacon. Brown onion and mushrooms in the bacon drippings. Remove and combine with bacon. Cut pork into 1/2-inch-thick pieces. Season with salt and pepper. Dip chops in beaten egg and then in the breadcrumbs. Brown in remaining bacon drippings. Fill a 1-quart casserole dish with alternate layers of meat and vegetables. Add liquid. Cover. Bake at 350° for 30 minutes. Yield: 4 servings.

CHEDDAR CHOPS CASSEROLE

       6 pork chops, 1 inch thick
       2 cups thinly sliced onion
       1 cup chopped green pepper
       1 cup uncooked regular rice
       2 cups water
       1 teaspoon salt
       1 (16-ounce) can tomatoes
     1/2 cup water
       1 teaspoon salt
     1/4 teaspoon pepper
       6 thin slices Cheddar cheese
           (about 1/2 pound)

Trim fat from pork chops. Render fat in a large skillet. Add chops and brown slowly on both sides. Remove chops from skillet, and add onion and green pepper to skillet. Cook for about 15 minutes, or until onions are tender.

Cook rice in boiling salted water according to package directions. Place cooked rice in the bottom of a greased 12- x 8- x 2-inch baking dish. Top with onion and green pepper; arrange browned chops on top. Spoon tomatoes over chops; add water, salt, and pepper. Cover dish with a lid or heavy-duty aluminum foil. Bake at 350° for 1 hour. Uncover, and add water if mixture has cooked dry. Lower oven temperature to 300°. Place slices of cheese on top of pork chops and bake at 300° for about 15 minutes, or until cheese melts. Yield: 6 servings.

PORK CHOP-VEGETABLE CASSEROLE

       8 pork chops
     1/2 cup chopped onion
     1/2 cup chopped green pepper
       1 (10-3/4-ounce) can cream of
           mushroom soup
       1 cup water
       3 cups cooked regular rice
       2 cups cooked green peas
       1 teaspoon salt
     1/8 teaspoon pepper

Place pork chops in a skillet and brown on both sides. Remove chops from skillet. Place onion and green pepper in the skillet and cook until tender. Add a small amount of shortening if needed to cook the onion and pepper. Add mushroom soup, water, rice, peas, salt, and pepper. Mix well. Pour half the rice and pea mixture into a greased 2-quart baking dish. Arrange half the pork chops over the rice and peas. Add the rest of the rice and peas, and top with the remaining pork chops. Bake at 350° for 30 minutes. Yield: 8 servings.

SAVORY PORK CHOPS EN CASSEROLE

       2 large onions, sliced
     1/4 cup butter or margarine
       1 (20-ounce) can tomatoes
       2 teaspoons sugar
       1 teaspoon salt
     1/4 teaspoon pepper
           Pinch oregano
       1 cup soft breadcrumbs
       2 cups canned applesauce
     1/4 cup prepared horseradish
       1 (20-ounce) can sauerkraut, drained
       6 pork chops, 1 inch thick
           Salt and pepper

Sauté onions in butter; add tomatoes, sugar, salt, pepper, oregano, and breadcrumbs. Combine applesauce and horseradish; mix well. Combine tomato mixture, applesauce mixture, and sauerkraut. Place in a greased 2-quart casserole dish. Sauté pork chops until golden brown. Lay chops on top of the sauerkraut mixture and sprinkle with salt and pepper. Cover and bake at 375° for 1 hour and 40 minutes, or until chops are tender. Yield: 6 servings.

CHEESE AND HAM CASSEROLE

    1 tablespoon butter or margarine
    1 tablespoon all-purpose flour
    2 cups milk, divided
  1/4 pound shredded Cheddar cheese
    4 eggs, well beaten
      Salt and cayenne or black pepper
      to taste
    2 tablespoons minced stuffed olives
    1 tablespoon minced parsley
    1 tablespoon minced green onion tops
  1/2 cup chopped ham
  1/2 cup mushroom pieces
      Sliced olives or parsley sprigs
      for garnish

Melt butter in a small pan; add flour and cook until flour has darkened. Gradually add 1 cup milk, stirring constantly. Stir in shredded cheese and cook over low heat until cheese has melted. Remove from heat and add 1 cup milk, eggs, salt, and pepper. Add minced olives, parsley, green onion, chopped ham, and mushroom pieces. Spoon into 6 or 8 well-greased individual baking dishes.

Place baking dishes in a pan with about 1 inch cold water in the pan. For earthenware dishes, bake at 375°, and for glass dishes, bake at 350° for 20 to 30 minutes, or until mixture is done. Insert knife blade into center of dishes, and if blade comes out clean, mixture is done. Serve hot, garnished with sliced olives or parsley sprigs. Yield: 6 to 8 servings.

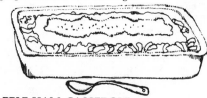

APPLE-HAM CASSEROLE

    3 cups diced cooked ham
    2 tablespoons prepared mustard
    2 apples, cored and sliced
    2 tablespoons freshly squeezed
      lemon juice
  1/2 cup brown sugar
    1 teaspoon grated orange rind
    2 tablespoons all-purpose flour

Arrange ham in a 1-1/2-quart casserole dish. Spread with mustard. Arrange cored and sliced apples over ham. Sprinkle with lemon juice. Combine brown sugar, orange rind, and flour; sprinkle over ham. Bake at 350° for 30 to 35 minutes. Yield: 4 servings.

HAM AND CORN CASSEROLE

  1/2 cup diced cooked ham
    1 (8-ounce) can cream-style corn
    2 tablespoons shredded Cheddar cheese
    1 egg, beaten
  1/2 cup milk
  1/2 cup cracker crumbs

Mix all ingredients together. Place in a greased 1-1/2-quart casserole dish and bake at 325° for about 45 minutes or until firm. Yield: 2 servings.

HAM SCALLOP

    4 medium sweet potatoes
    2 cups canned applesauce
  1/4 cup brown sugar
  1/2 teaspoon ground nutmeg
    1 (1-1/4-pound) ham slice
    1 teaspoon dry mustard
    3 tablespoons brown sugar
  1/2 teaspoon ground nutmeg
    3 tablespoons vinegar

Pare sweet potatoes and halve lengthwise. Combine applesauce, sugar, and 1/2 teaspoon nutmeg. Arrange alternate layers of sweet potatoes and applesauce mixture in a greased, flat casserole dish; place ham slice on top. Cover and bake at 350° for 1 hour, or until sweet potatoes and ham are tender. About 20 minutes before casserole is done, make a topping for the ham by combining the dry mustard, brown sugar, 1/2 teaspoon nutmeg, and vinegar. Spread on top of ham. Yield: 4 to 6 servings.

ASPARAGUS CASSEROLE WITH HAM

    2 tablespoons butter or margarine
    1 tablespoon all-purpose flour
    1 (10-3/4-ounce) can cream of
      mushroom soup
  1/4 teaspoon prepared mustard
    1 (14-1/2-ounce) can asparagus
    1 (17-ounce) can green peas
    4 hard-cooked eggs, sliced
    1 cup chopped cooked ham
  1/2 cup buttered breadcrumbs
  1/4 cup shredded cheese

Blend butter and flour in a saucepan. Add mushroom soup and cook until thick; stir in mustard. Combine the asparagus, peas, eggs, and ham in a greased 2-quart casserole dish; pour mushroom sauce over all. Mix breadcrumbs with cheese. Spread over top of the casserole. Bake at 300° for 30 minutes, or until casserole is brown and bubbly. Yield: 4 to 6 servings.

COMPANY CASSEROLE

8 hard-cooked eggs
1/4 cup melted butter or margarine
1/2 teaspoon Worcestershire sauce
1/4 teaspoon prepared mustard
1 teaspoon finely chopped parsley
1 teaspoon chopped chives
1/3 cup finely chopped cooked ham
3 tablespoons butter or margarine
3 tablespoons all-purpose flour
1 cup chicken broth
3/4 cup milk
Dash salt and pepper
1 cup shredded American cheese

Cut hard-cooked eggs in half lengthwise; remove and mash yolks. Mix yolks with 1/4 cup melted butter, Worcestershire sauce, mustard, parsley, chives, and ham. Fill egg whites with this mixture. Arrange filled egg halves in a greased, flat 1-1/2- to 2-quart baking dish.

To prepare white sauce, melt 3 tablespoons butter in a saucepan. Blend in flour and cook until bubbly. Add chicken broth, milk, and seasonings. Cook over low heat, stirring constantly, until mixture is smooth and thickened throughout. Pour sauce over egg halves. Sprinkle with shredded cheese. Bake at 350° for 20 minutes, or until cheese is melted. Yield: 4 to 6 servings.

HAM AND ARTICHOKE CASSEROLE

4 tablespoons butter or margarine
4 tablespoons all-purpose flour
2 cups warm milk
Generous dash seasoned salt
Generous dash cayenne pepper
1/4 teaspoon ground nutmeg
Paprika
Pinch white pepper
1/3 cup shredded Swiss cheese and 1/3 cup grated Parmesan cheese, mixed
4 tablespoons dry sherry
2 (1-pound) cans artichoke hearts, drained
12 thin slices boiled or baked ham
Topping

Melt butter in a saucepan over medium heat; blend in flour; when mixture is smooth, remove from heat. Gradually stir in warm milk; when smooth return to heat. Stir constantly until thickened. Add seasonings, then cheese; stir over low heat until melted. Remove from heat and stir in sherry.

If artichoke hearts are large, cut in half and wrap two halves in a slice of ham, allowing two ham rolls per person. Arrange ham rolls in a buttered casserole dish with sides of the rolls touching; pour sauce over all. Sprinkle with Topping and bake at 350° for 25 to 30 minutes, or until brown and bubbly. Yield: 6 servings.

Note: You may not need two cans of artichoke hearts. The size of the artichokes varies according to the processor. It is best to buy two, then open one and see.

Topping

2/3 cup buttered breadcrumbs
1/3 cup grated Parmesan cheese mixed with 1/3 cup shredded Swiss cheese

Combine breadcrumbs and cheese mixture and sprinkle over casserole.

HAM AND ASPARAGUS CASSEROLE

1 (10-ounce) package frozen cut asparagus
2 cups diced cooked ham
1/4 cup shredded American cheese
2 tablespoons quick-cooking tapioca
2 tablespoons chopped green pepper
2 tablespoons chopped onion
1 tablespoon minced parsley
1 tablespoon freshly squeezed lemon juice
2 hard-cooked eggs, sliced
1/2 cup milk
1 (10-3/4-ounce) can cream of mushroom soup
2 tablespoons melted butter or margarine
1/2 cup coarse dry breadcrumbs

Cook asparagus until tender. Drain thoroughly and arrange in a greased 1-1/2-quart casserole dish. Combine ham, cheese, tapioca, green pepper, onion, parsley, and lemon juice. Cover asparagus with half of the ham mixture, then egg slices; top with remaining ham mixture. Combine milk with mushroom soup and pour over the casserole. Mix melted butter with breadcrumbs; sprinkle over the top. Bake at 375° for 25 to 30 minutes, or until crumbs are lightly browned. Yield: 5 to 6 servings.

HAM AND NOODLE CASSEROLE

- 1 cup uncooked wide noodles
- 1/2 cup evaporated milk
- 1/2 cup water
- 2 eggs, beaten
- 1/2 teaspoon salt
- 1-1/2 cups cooked chopped ham
- 1/2 teaspoon paprika
- 4 tablespoons butter or margarine
- 1/2 cup chopped green pepper
- 1 tablespoon grated onion
- 1 cup buttered breadcrumbs

Break noodles into short lengths. Cook in a large quantity of boiling salted water until noodles are tender; drain. Combine drained noodles with milk, water, eggs, salt, ham, paprika, butter, green pepper, and onion. Mix well and place mixture in a buttered 2-quart casserole dish. Cover with buttered breadcrumbs and bake at 350° for about 40 minutes. Yield: 8 servings.

Variations: Chopped beef or chicken may be substituted for the ham, and drained sliced mushrooms may be added.

HAM AND RICE CASSEROLE

- 2 (10-3/4-ounce) cans cream of celery soup
- 1 cup light cream
- 1 cup shredded Cheddar cheese
- 1/2 cup grated Parmesan cheese
- 1-1/2 tablespoons minced onion
- 1 tablespoon prepared mustard
- 1 teaspoon grated lemon rind
- 1/4 teaspoon ground rosemary
- 1/8 teaspoon pepper
- 4 cups cooked rice
- 4 cups cubed cooked ham
- 1 (20-ounce) can cut green beans
- 1 (3-1/2-ounce) can French fried onion rings

Combine celery soup and cream; stir until smooth; heat slowly until hot, being careful not to boil. Stir in cheeses. Then blend in onion, mustard, lemon rind, rosemary, and pepper. Remove from heat. Combine sauce with rice and ham. Alternate layers of ham and rice mixture with green beans in a greased 3-quart casserole dish, ending with ham and rice mixture. Sprinkle with French fried onion rings. Bake, uncovered, at 350° for 15 to 20 minutes, or until bubbly. Yield: 10 servings.

Note: If your family is small, freeze half of this for later serving.

PLANTATION CASSEROLE

- 2 cups chopped cooked ham, chicken, or beef
- 1-1/2 cups cooked peas, drained
- 1 (1-pound) can cream-style corn
- 1/4 pound American Cheese, cubed
- 1 cup evaporated milk, divided
- 1/4 cup chopped onion
- 1 tablespoon Worcestershire sauce
- 1 cup biscuit mix
- 1/2 cup cornmeal
- 2 tablespoons sugar
- 1/2 teaspoon salt
- 1 egg, beaten

Mix meat, peas, corn, cubed cheese, 1/3 cup evaporated milk, onion, and Worcestershire sauce. Pour into a greased 12- x 8- x 2-inch baking dish. Bake at 400° for 10 minutes, or until mixture is bubbly around edges. Combine biscuit mix, cornmeal, sugar, salt, and beaten egg. Add remaining milk and mix well. Pour around edges of hot meat mixture, leaving center uncovered. Bake for 20 minutes longer. Yield: 6 servings.

EASY SAUSAGE CASSEROLE

- 24 small sausage links (about 2 pounds)
- 2 tablespoons drippings
- 2 tablespoons all-purpose flour
- 1 cup milk
- 1 (29-ounce) can hominy, drained and liquid reserved
  Salt and pepper to taste
- 1/2 teaspoon marjoram
- 1/2 cup chopped celery
  Paprika

Fry sausage links until deep golden brown. Remove; drain all but 2 tablespoons drippings from skillet. To this, add flour and stir well. Add milk and liquid from the can of hominy and make a gravy. Add hominy, salt, pepper, marjoram, celery, and sausage. Mix and pour into a 3-quart casserole dish; sprinkle with paprika. Cover and bake at 400° for about 10 minutes: Yield: 4 to 6 servings.

CORN AND SAUSAGE CASSEROLE

    4 eggs
    1 (1-pound) can cream-style corn
    1 teaspoon salt
1/4 teaspoon pepper
    1 cup soft breadcrumbs
    1 pound pork sausage
1/2 cup cracker crumbs

Beat eggs; add corn, salt, pepper, breadcrumbs, and sausage. Place in a greased 2- to 3-quart casserole dish. Add cracker crumbs on top. Bake, uncovered, at 350° for 50 minutes. Yield: 6 to 8 servings.

SAUSAGE-BEAN BAKE

1/4 cup molasses
    3 tablespoons prepared mustard
    2 tablespoons vinegar or freshly
      squeezed lemon juice
    2 teaspoons Worcestershire sauce
1/4 teaspoon hot pepper sauce
    2 (1-pound) cans baked beans
    2 cups cooked apple slices
    1 pound pork link sausage

Combine molasses and mustard; stir in vinegar, Worcestershire sauce, and hot pepper sauce. Turn baked beans and apple slices into a 1-1/2-quart casserole dish; stir in molasses mixture. Bake at 450° for 30 minutes. While beans are cooking, place sausage links in a cold skillet. Cook over low heat for 12 to 15 minutes, turning often until browned. Pour off fat as it accumulates. To serve, place sausage on top of beans. Yield: 8 to 10 servings.

SAUSAGE-BEAN CASSEROLE

1/2 pound dried lima beans
    1 pint hot water
    2 teaspoons salt
    2 cups canned tomatoes
    2 pounds sausage links
    2 tablespoons water
    2 tablespoons sausage drippings
    1 small onion, sliced
    1 tablespoon all-purpose flour
    1 teaspoon dry mustard
    1 tablespoon sugar
1/8 teaspoon pepper

Cover beans with water and soak overnight. Drain. Add hot water and salt; cook until just tender, about 1 hour. Add tomatoes and continue cooking for 1 hour.

Place sausage links and 2 tablespoons water in a cold frying pan. Cover and cook slowly for 8 to 10 minutes. Remove cover and brown links. Remove links; pour off all but 2 tablespoons drippings. Brown onion in drippings. Blend in flour and add remaining ingredients. Combine with beans. Add sausage links to mixture and simmer for 10 minutes. Yield: 8 to 10 servings.

SAUSAGE CASSEROLE

    1 pound mild sausage
1/2 pound hot sausage
1-1/2 cups chopped celery
    2 medium onions, chopped
    1 large green pepper, chopped
    1 (16-ounce) can tomatoes
    1 (8-ounce) package shell macaroni
    1 (16-ounce) can English peas

Crumble sausage in a heavy skillet and cook until brown. Add celery, onion, and green pepper, and cook until transparent. Transfer to a large saucepan and add the tomatoes; cover and simmer for 2 hours. Add macaroni and peas; cover and cook slowly for 45 minutes, or until macaroni is tender. Stir often, but carefully, so macaroni will not be broken. Add water if mixture becomes too thick. Skim off excess fat before serving. Yield: 10 to 12 servings.

Note: To freeze, cut down on cooking time of vegetables and macaroni. Place into two 2-quart casserole dishes; seal and freeze. Remove from freezer, thaw, then cook for about 30 minutes, or until mixture is thoroughly heated.

SAUSAGE-SWEET POTATO CASSEROLE

    4 cups thinly sliced sweet potatoes
    4 cups thinly sliced tart apples
    2 teaspoons dehydrated onion flakes
    2 teaspoons salt
3/4 cup maple-blended syrup
3/4 cup apple cider
1/2 cup melted butter or margarine
   12 brown-and-serve pork sausage

Arrange alternate layers of sweet potatoes and apple slices in a greased 2-quart casserole dish, sprinkling each layer with onion and salt. Combine syrup, cider, and melted butter, and pour over all. Cover; bake at 350° for 1 hour. Arrange sausages on top; bake, uncovered, 15 to 20 minutes longer, or until sausages are brown and apples and sweet potatoes are tender. Yield: 6 servings.

VARIETY MEATS CASSEROLES

CORNED BEEF CASSEROLE

    1 (8-ounce) package macaroni
    1 (10-3/4-ounce) can cream of
        chicken soup
    1 (12-ounce) can corned beef,
        cut into small pieces
    1 cup milk
 1/4 pound Cheddar cheese, shredded
    1 small onion, chopped
        Buttered breadcrumbs

Cook macaroni according to package directions. Drain. Combine with soup, corned beef, milk, cheese, and onion. Place into a greased 1-1/2-quart casserole dish, and top with breadcrumbs. Bake at 350° for about 30 minutes, or until crumbs are browned. Yield: 6 to 8 servings.

Caraway

Caraway, the rye bread and cheese seed, adds piquant flavor to noodles, sauerkraut, and cheese. Caraway seed is a flavorful addition to seafood, beet, potato, or cabbage casseroles.

EAST INDIAN BEEF

    2 cups 1/2-inch bread cubes
    2 tablespoons butter or margarine, melted
 1/4 pound dried beef, cut into pieces
        Cold water
    3 tablespoons butter or margarine
    3 tablespoons all-purpose flour
    1 teaspoon curry powder
    2 cups milk
    2 (6-ounce) cans mushroom sauce
    1 cup shredded sharp cheese
    1 (7-ounce) package spaghetti, cooked

Toss bread cubes with 2 tablespoons melted butter. If dried beef is salty, soak in cold water for about 30 minutes. Drain. Melt 3 tablespoons butter in a saucepan or skillet. Sauté dried beef until lightly browned. Blend in flour and curry powder. Combine milk and mushroom sauce. Add all at once to dried beef mixture. Stir constantly until sauce thickens and boils, about 1 minute. Remove from heat. Blend in cheese, stirring until melted. Arrange alternate layers of spaghetti and dried beef mixture in a greased 1-1/2-quart shallow baking dish, ending with beef mixture. Top with bread cubes. Bake at 375° for 20 minutes, or until mixture is bubbly. Yield: 6 servings.

YANKEE DOODLE DANDY

1-1/2 cups diagonally sliced celery
 1/4 cup butter or margarine, melted
    2 tablespoons all-purpose flour
 1/2 teaspoon salt
    1 cup milk
    1 (17-ounce) can cream-style corn
    1 (8-ounce) package noodles,
        cooked and drained
    1 cup shredded sharp Cheddar cheese
 1/4 pound shredded dried beef

Sauté celery in melted butter until just tender. Stir in flour and salt; gradually blend in milk. Add corn, and combine mixture with cooked noodles. Add cheese and dried beef. Mix well and place in a greased 2-1/2-quart casserole dish. Bake at 350° for about 30 minutes. Yield: 6 to 8 servings.

Thyme

Thyme should be used with a light touch because of its strong distinctive flavor. Thyme adapts to beef, game, lamb, veal, fish, and pork dishes. It adds an interesting flavor to cheese and vegetable casseroles.

BAKED MACARONI AND CORNED BEEF

  1 cup uncooked elbow macaroni
  1 (10-3/4-ounce) can cream of
    mushroom soup
  1 cup milk
  1 teaspoon prepared mustard
1/2 cup shredded sharp cheese
1/4 cup chopped celery
1/4 cup sliced stuffed olives
  1 (12-ounce) can corned beef,
    unchilled, and flaked

Cook macaroni according to package directions; drain. Combine soup, milk, and mustard. Add macaroni and remaining ingredients. Pour into a greased 1-1/2-quart casserole dish. Bake at 350° for 25 minutes. Yield: 4 servings.

STEWED GROUSE

  2 grouse (not too young)
  2 tablespoons all-purpose flour
  1 teaspoon salt
1/4 teaspoon pepper
1/4 teaspoon onion salt
1/4 teaspoon celery salt
1/2 teaspoon monosodium glutamate
  2 tablespoons bacon drippings, or
    butter or margarine
  2 medium onions, thinly sliced
  2 medium carrots, thinly sliced
1/4 pound mushrooms, sliced
  1 bay leaf
  6 small link sausages
  1 tablespoon whiskey (optional)
  2 chicken bouillon cubes
1-1/2 cups boiling water

Cut grouse into quarters. Combine flour and seasonings, and sprinkle over grouse. Sauté over low heat in the bacon drippings. Line the bottom of the buttered casserole dish with the sliced onions, carrots, and mushrooms; place browned grouse on top of the vegetables. Next add the bay leaf, sausages, whiskey, and bouillon cubes dissolved in boiling water. Cover with a very tight lid. Bake at 325° for 2 hours. Stir well before serving. Yield: 4 to 6 servings.

DOVE HASH A LA REITH

  4 cups diced, cooked breast of doves
  1 (10-1/2-ounce) can chicken consommé
  6 tablespoons butter or margarine, divided
2-1/2 tablespoons all-purpose flour
2/3 cup cream
2/3 cup breadcrumbs
2/3 cup chopped green pepper
2/3 cup chopped onion
  2 tablespoons chopped parsley
1/2 teaspoon ground sage
1/2 teaspoon salt
    Pepper to taste
1/4 cup sherry

Cook whole doves in chicken consommé until tender. Remove breasts and dice meat; measure 4 cups and set aside. Blend 3 tablespoons butter with flour and cream. Sauté breadcrumbs, green pepper, onion, parsley, and sage in the remaining 3 tablespoons butter. Mix the sautéed ingredients, flour mixture, and dove meat. Add salt, pepper, and sherry; let cook gently for 25 to 30 minutes. Before serving, place in a greased casserole dish and cook for a few minutes under the broiler. To keep the right consistency while sautéing, add pot liquor left from cooking whole doves. Yield: 4 to 6 servings.

DOVE PIE

  6 doves
  4 cups water
  1 onion, chopped
  1 small bunch parsley, chopped
  3 whole cloves
  2 tablespoons all-purpose flour
  2 tablespoons butter or margarine
    Salt and pepper
    Pastry for 2 piecrusts

Place doves in a saucepan; cover with water; add onion, parsley, and cloves. Cook until tender. Remove doves. Skim liquid and thicken with a paste made of flour and butter. Season to taste with salt and pepper. Line a baking dish with pastry and place birds in dish. Cover with gravy. Top with pastry. Bake at 350° for 1 hour. Yield: 4 to 6 servings.

Mint

Mint's strong, sweet flavor makes it one of the most popular herbs. It adds an interesting flavor to lamb dishes and is a nice addition to casseroles of beans, peas, spinach, or carrots.

FRANKS AND CHEESE CASSEROLE

1-2/3 cups evaporated milk
  1/2 teaspoon salt
    2 cups shredded cheese
    4 cups cooked noodles
    2 cups sliced frankfurters

Simmer evaporated milk and salt over low heat to just below the boiling point. Add cheese and stir until melted. Place cooked noodles and frankfurters in a buttered 2-quart casserole dish; pour cheese mixture on top. Bake at 350° for 30 minutes. Yield: 4 to 6 servings.

CANNED MEAT CASSEROLE

    1 (12-ounce) can luncheon meat
    1 cup fine breadcrumbs
  1/4 cup evaporated milk
    2 medium onions
    4 tablespoons all-purpose flour
    3 tablespoons butter or margarine
    1 (8-1/2-ounce) can green peas,
      drained and liquid reserved
2-1/2 cups sliced potatoes
      Liquid from peas plus enough water to
      make 1 cup
  1/4 teaspoon salt
      Dash pepper

Shred or chop luncheon meat. Add breadcrumbs and milk; blend well. Chop 1 onion very fine and blend into the meat mixture. Shape mixture into 12 balls and coat well with flour.

Melt butter; add other onion, thinly sliced, and cook gently until transparent. Remove onion and save. Brown meatballs. Arrange meatballs, cooked onion, peas, and potatoes in two layers each in a greased 2-quart casserole dish. Add drippings from frying the meat. Add liquid and seasonings. Bake at 375° for about 10 minutes. Yield: 6 servings.

CABALLERO CASSEROLE

    2 (15-ounce) cans tamales
    2 (12-ounce) cans whole kernel corn
      with sweet peppers
    1 (14-ounce) can pizza sauce
      Cheese Olive Topping

Cut each tamale into 6 slices and place half into the bottom of a 11- x 9- x 2-inch baking dish. Spread with 1 can corn; top with remaining tamale slices and corn. Pour pizza sauce over all. Spoon Cheese Olive Topping over casserole. Bake at 400° for 30 minutes. Yield: 8 servings.

Cheese Olive Topping

  1/2 cup all-purpose flour
  3/4 cup cornmeal
    1 (0.5-ounce) envelope cheese sauce mix
1-1/2 teaspoons baking powder
    1 teaspoon salt
    1 egg, slighty beaten
  3/4 cup milk
  1/4 cup salad oil
    2 tablespoons chopped ripe olives

In a large mixing bowl, combine flour, cornmeal, cheese sauce mix, baking powder, and salt; add remaining ingredients. Stir until a dough is formed. Spoon over casserole. Yield: about 2-1/2 cups.

CASSEROLE OF RICE AND LAMB

    2 cups cooked rice, divided
    2 cups chopped cooked lamb
  1/2 teaspoon salt
  1/8 teaspoon celery salt
  1/8 teaspoon paprika
    1 egg, slightly beaten
    1 cup breadcrumbs
      Milk to moisten
      Butter or margarine

Line the bottom of a greased 1-1/2-quart casserole dish with half of the cooked rice. To the lamb, add seasonings, egg, crumbs, and milk; place into the casserole dish. Cover the meat with the remaining rice. Place bits of butter on top. Cover casserole dish, and place in a pan of water. Bake at 325° for 45 minutes. Yield: 4 to 6 servings.

CURRIED LAMB

    1 (2-pound) shoulder of lamb
    3 tablespoons all-purpose flour
    3 tablespoons shortening
    1 small onion, sliced
    1 teaspoon curry powder
    1 teaspoon freshly squeezed lemon juice
1/2 cup boiling water
1/2 cup tomato juice
    1 teaspoon salt
      Cooked rice

Cut lamb into 1-inch cubes. Dredge with flour and brown in shortening in a heavy Dutch oven. Add all other ingredients except rice; simmer slowly until meat is tender. Serve over hot, cooked rice. Yield: 6 servings.

LAMB RISOTTO CASSEROLE

1/2 lemon
    4 thick lamb chops
3/4 cup uncooked brown rice
    1 (10-1/2-ounce) can consommé
    2 carrots, cut in julienne strips
  10 small pearl onions
    1 cup Sauterne
1/4 teaspoon ground marjoram
1/8 teaspoon oregano
1/2 teaspoon salt
      Dash pepper

Squeeze lemon over chops; set aside. Place brown rice, consommé, carrots, onions, and Sauterne wine in a large casserole dish. Arrange lamb chops on top. Cover and bake at 350° for 30 minutes. Remove from oven, add seasonings, and stir. Return to oven and bake 30 minutes longer. Yield: 4 servings.

TONGUE AND SCALLOPED CORN

    2 tablespoons chopped onion
    2 tablespoons butter or margarine
    2 tablespoons all-purpose flour
    1 cup milk
1/8 teaspoon ground nutmeg
    1 cup diced, cooked smoked tongue
    2 cups cooked whole kernel corn, drained
1/4 cup breadcrumbs
    2 tablespoons butter or margarine, melted

Panfry onion in butter. Stir in flour; add milk and nutmeg. Cook until mixture boils. Combine tongue, sauce, and corn in a greased 1-1/2-quart baking dish. Combine breadcrumbs and butter. Sprinkle over casserole. Bake at 350° for 25 to 30 minutes. Yield: 4 servings.

LIVER AND RICE CASSEROLE

    1 pound sliced liver,
      cut into 1-inch squares
1/4 cup chopped green pepper
1/2 cup chopped celery
    1 medium onion, diced
    2 tablespoons salad oil
    1 (8-ounce) can tomato sauce
    1 (16-ounce) can tomatoes
1-1/2 teaspoons salt
1/2 teaspoon pepper
1/8 teaspoon thyme
    3 cups cooked rice
1/2 cup shredded sharp Cheddar cheese

Cook liver, green pepper, celery, and onion in salad oil until liver is very lightly browned and vegetables are tender. Pour off fat. Add tomato sauce, tomatoes, salt, pepper, thyme, and rice. Pour into a greased 1-1/2-quart casserole dish. Sprinkle shredded cheese over the top and bake at 350° for 20 to 30 minutes. Yield: 4 to 5 servings.

BAKED LIVER WITH APPLES

    1 pound beef liver, sliced
    2 medium apples, chopped
    1 medium onion, chopped
1-1/2 teaspoons salt
1/8 teaspoon pepper
    6 slices bacon, cut into pieces
1/4 cup water or beef bouillon

Place liver into a greased shallow casserole dish. Cover with apples, onion, salt, and pepper. Top with bacon pieces and add liquid. Bake, covered, at 325° for 1-1/2 hours; remove cover during the last 20 minutes of baking. Yield: 6 servings.

OYSTER-STUFFED DOVE PIE

    16 doves
     2 cups chopped celery
     1 cup chopped onion
     3 slices bacon, chopped
       Salt and pepper to taste
     4 cups water
     4 dozen oysters
     4 tablespoons all-purpose flour
    1/4 cup water
       Pastry for 2 piecrusts

Have doves picked and drawn; do not split open. Wash doves in cold water and dry. Keep in refrigerator for several days. When ready to cook, place doves in a heavy pot and add celery, onion, bacon, salt, and pepper; cover with water 3 inches above birds. Bring to a boil; reduce heat, stir, and cover. Simmer for about 30 minutes, or until doves are tender. Remove from heat. Place each bird on a flat pan. When cool enough to handle, drain oysters, and stuff as many as possible into each dove.

Mix flour with 1/4 cup water to make a paste, then add enough liquid from pot to blend well. Add this to the pot in which doves were cooked; place over low heat and stir constantly until thickened to about the consistency of cream. Add the remaining oysters and remove from heat.

Line bottom and sides of a casserole dish with 1/2 of the flaky pastry and bake at 350° for about 10 minutes to set pastry. Remove from oven and cool. Put in a layer of doves, then a layer of liquid with oysters. Repeat until casserole is within 1/2 inch of the top. Cover with remaining pastry. Prick top of pastry and bake at 350° until pastry is golden brown. Serve hot. Yield: 8 servings.

SMOTHERED QUAIL

     6 quail
     6 tablespoons melted butter or margarine
     3 tablespoons all-purpose flour
     2 cups chicken broth
    1/2 cup sherry
       Salt and pepper to taste
       Cooked rice

Prepare quail; brown in a heavy skillet or Dutch oven in butter. Remove quail to a baking dish. Add flour to butter in skillet and stir well. Slowly add chicken broth and sherry; salt and pepper to taste. Blend well and pour over quail. Cover and bake at 350° for about 1 hour. Serve with cooked rice. Yield: 6 servings.

QUAIL WITH WILD RICE

    10 quail
    1-1/4 cups melted butter or margarine, divided
    1-1/2 pounds chicken livers
       2 large onions, chopped
       1 green pepper, chopped
       2 cloves garlic, minced
    2-1/2 cups cooked wild rice
       2 cups chicken broth
    1-1/2 cups Port

Sew together body cavity of quail. Sauté quail in 1/2 cup butter until browned. Place in a baking dish, cover and bake at 325° for about 30 minutes.

Sauté livers, onion, pepper, and garlic in 3/4 cup butter. Do not let vegetables brown, but cook to a clear color. Add cooked rice, chicken broth, and wine. Place mixture in a 3-quart baking dish; cover and bake at 325° for about 20 minutes, or until liquid is absorbed. Serve quail over rice. Yield: 8 to 10 servings.

Variation: Body cavity of quail may be sewed up and the quail lightly browned in butter and placed on top of the stuffing in a baking pan. Mix chicken broth and wine; pour over quail and stuffing. Cover pan and bake at 375° for about 30 minutes.

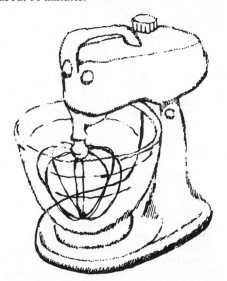

Rosemary

Rosemary is a sweet and fresh-tasting herb. Lightly used, it adds a mild flavor to lamb, beef, veal, game, and fish casseroles. It is excellent in vegetable dishes — peas, spinach, and cauliflower.

QUAIL PIE

- 6 quail
- 2 cups water
- 3 cups self-rising flour
- 1 cup shortening
  Ice water
  Salt and pepper to taste
- 3 tablespoons melted butter
- 2 tablespoons all-purpose flour
  Milk

Cook quail in water in a pressure cooker for about 25 minutes. Make a pastry of flour, shortening, and just enough ice water to make a stiff dough. Roll out 1/2 of the pastry to cover the bottom of a large casserole dish. Remove quail from cooker, and save the broth. Remove bones from quail and place meat in the casserole dish. Sprinkle with salt and pepper; pour melted butter evenly over the meat. Thicken broth with 2 tablespoons flour and pour over quail. Roll remaining pastry thin and cut into strips. All pastry strips should be well pricked. Place a few thin, pricked strips of pastry over the quail, bringing ends of strips to meet bottom pastry. Brush with milk and bake at 350° for 40 minutes. Yield: 4 servings.

CORN 'N FRANKS

- 1/3 cup chopped onion
- 5 tablespoons butter or margarine
- 1/3 cup sliced green pepper
- 2 (12-ounce) cans whole kernel
  yellow corn
- 2/3 cup pitted black olives
- 1/3 cup shredded Swiss cheese
- 6 beef frankfurters
- 1/3 cup tomato puree
  Grated Parmesan cheese

Sauté onion in butter. Add green pepper and sauté until tender. Drain liquid from corn and olives. Add corn and olives to onion and pepper. Stir in Swiss cheese. Place in a greased 1-1/2-quart baking dish; place frankfurters, slashed diagonally, over the corn mixture. Top with tomato puree and a sprinkling of Parmesan cheese. Bake at 350° for 25 minutes. Yield: 6 servings.

Marjoram

Marjoram, an herb of the mint family, is a perfect complement to lamb and veal dishes. This versatile herb is excellent in meat and seafood casseroles and combines well with spinach, peas, and green bean dishes.

FRANK-CORN MUFFIN CASSEROLE

- 1/4 cup butter or margarine
- 1 tablespoon chopped onion
- 3 tablespoons all-purpose flour
- 1 tablespoon prepared mustard
- 1/2 teaspoon salt
- 2 cups milk
- 1 pound frankfurters,
  cut into 1-inch pieces
- 1 (10-ounce) package frozen peas,
  or 2 cups canned peas
- 1 (12-ounce) package corn muffin mix

Melt the butter; add onion and brown lightly. Blend in flour, mustard, and salt; slowly add milk. Stir and cook until thickened. Add frankfurters and peas; heat until boiling. Pour into a greased 13- x 9- x 2-inch baking dish.

Prepare corn muffin batter according to package directions. Drop the batter by tablespoonsful along the edges of the hot frankfurter mixture. Bake at 375° for 30 minutes, or until topping is golden brown. Yield: 6 servings.

CHILDREN'S DELIGHT CASSEROLE

- 1 pound frankfurters, chopped
- 1 (5.3-ounce) can evaporated milk
- 1 (10-3/4-ounce) can cream of
  chicken soup
- 1 (10-3/4-ounce) can cream of celery soup
- 1 (5-ounce) can chow mein noodles

Mix all ingredients together. Bake in a buttered 1-quart casserole dish at 350° for 25 minutes. Yield: 6 servings.

POTATO 'N FRANK CASSEROLE

- 1 (12-ounce) package frozen potato patties
- 3 frankfurters, sliced
- 2 tablespoons finely chopped onion
  Dash salt
  Dash pepper
- 3/4 cup milk
- 1 tablespoon butter or margarine

Arrange the frozen patties, sliced franks, and chopped onion in layers in a greased 1-1/2-quart casserole dish. Sprinkle with salt and pepper; pour milk over the top, and dot with butter. Cover and bake at 350° for about 1 hour, or until the potatoes are tender. Stir with a fork to break up potato patties after 15 minutes of baking and again 30 minutes later. Yield: 3 or 4 servings.

POULTRY CASSEROLES

CHICKEN AND RICE CRISP

    2 (10-3/4-ounce) cans cream of
       mushroom soup
    1 cup half-and-half
    1 cup shredded sharp Cheddar cheese
  1/2 cup grated Parmesan cheese
1-1/2 tablespoons minced onion
    1 tablespoon prepared mustard
  1/4 teaspoon rosemary
  1/8 teaspoon pepper
    4 cups cooked rice
    4 cups cubed, cooked chicken
    1 (1-pound 4-ounce) can carrots and peas
    1 (3-1/2-ounce) can French fried
       onion rings

Blend soup with half-and-half; cook over low heat until hot, being careful not to boil. Stir in cheeses, onion, and seasonings; remove from heat. Combine sauce, rice, and chicken. Alternate layers of the rice mixture with carrots and peas in a lightly buttered 3-quart casserole dish. Sprinkle top with onion rings. Bake, uncovered, at 350° for 15 to 20 minutes, or until the mixture is bubbly. Yield: 10 servings.

CHICKEN CASSOULET

    1 (3- to 4-pound) fryer chicken
  1/4 cup seasoned all-purpose flour
    6 tablespoons salad oil
    1 small onion, sliced
    1 clove garlic, minced
    4 stalks celery, cut into 1-inch slices
    4 carrots, cut into 1-inch slices
    1 green pepper, cut into 1-inch slices
  1/4 pound fresh mushrooms
  1/2 cup white wine (dry sherry or Sauterne)
    1 cup chicken broth or consommé
    1 teaspoon salt
    Pepper

Cut up chicken into serving-size pieces. Wash well. Place in a paper bag with flour; close bag and shake vigorously. Brown floured chicken well in salad oil. Place chicken in a greased 13- x 9- x 2-inch baking dish. Lightly sauté the onion, garlic, celery, carrots, green pepper, and mushrooms in oil left in the skillet; add to casserole with the chicken. Add wine and hot chicken broth. Sprinkle with salt and pepper. Cover tightly and bake at 325° for 1 hour, or until tender. Yield: 4 servings.

CHICKEN ENCHILADA CASSEROLE

    1 (4- to 5-pound) chicken
    1 large onion, diced
    2 cups chicken broth
    Salt and pepper to taste
    Crushed garlic (optional)
    2 (3- or 4-ounce) cans chopped green chiles
    1 (10-3/4-ounce) can cream of
       mushroom soup
    1 (10-3/4-ounce) can cream of celery soup
1-1/2 to 2 dozen tortillas
    1 pound Cheddar cheese, shredded

Cook chicken until tender. Remove from water, cool, and remove meat from bones. Cut into small pieces. Reserve broth in which chicken was cooked.

In a small amount of fat removed from cooled chicken broth, cook onion until slightly wilted. Add 2 cups chicken broth, salt, pepper, garlic, and chopped chicken. Add green chiles, mushroom and celery soups and heat thoroughly. Cut tortillas in quarters or leave whole. Arrange layers of tortillas, chicken mixture, and cheese in a greased 4- to 6-quart casserole dish. Cover; bake at 325° for 35 minutes. Yield: 8 to 12 servings.

CHICKEN-BROCCOLI BAKE

    2 chicken breasts
    2 tablespoons melted butter or margarine
    1 (10-ounce) package frozen broccoli,
      cooked and drained
    1 (10-3/4-ounce) can cream of
      chicken soup
    1/2 cup milk
    1/2 cup shredded American cheese
    1/4 cup breadcrumbs
      Paprika

Arrange chicken in a greased 8- x 4- x 2-inch baking dish. Drizzle butter over chicken. Bake at 375° for 40 minutes. Place cooked and drained broccoli around chicken. Blend soup, milk, and cheese; pour over chicken and broccoli. Top with breadcrumbs and sprinkle with paprika. Bake for 20 minutes longer. Yield: 2 servings.

CHICKEN CASSEROLE

    2 cups chopped cooked chicken
    2 (10-3/4-ounce) cans cream of
      chicken soup
    2 cups diced celery
    4 teaspoons minced onion
    1 cup chopped blanched almonds
    1 teaspoon salt
    1/2 teaspoon pepper
    2 tablespoons freshly squeezed lemon juice
1-1/2 cups mayonnaise or salad dressing
    6 hard-cooked eggs, sliced
    2 cups crushed potato chips

Combine cooked chicken, soup, celery, onion, almonds, salt, pepper, lemon juice, and mayonnaise in a large bowl and mix well. Spoon a layer of the mixture into a greased 3-quart casserole dish; add a layer of sliced eggs. Repeat layers. Cover with crushed potato chips and bake at 400° for 15 minutes. Yield: 8 servings.
    Note: This casserole may be prepared a day ahead and kept in the refrigerator. Do not add potato chips until ready to bake.

CHICKEN-RICE CASSEROLE

    1 cup uncooked regular rice
    1 (10-3/4-ounce) can cream of celery soup
    1 (10-3/4-ounce) can cream of
      chicken soup
    1 cup water
    6 chicken breasts
    1/4 cup melted butter or margarine

Place rice in the bottom of a greased 2-quart casserole dish. Mix soup with water and pour over rice. Dip chicken breasts in melted butter, then lay on top of the rice. Bake at 325° for about 45 minutes. Yield: 6 to 8 servings.

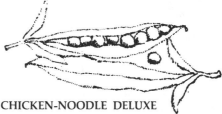

CHICKEN-NOODLE DELUXE

    1 (10-3/4-ounce) can cream of
      chicken soup
    1/3 cup commercial sour cream
    1/3 cup water
    1 cup diced, cooked chicken (5-ounce can
      boned chicken)
    2 tablespoons chopped pimiento
    1 tablespoon sherry
    2 cups cooked noodles (about 5 ounces
      uncooked)
      Water chestnuts, sliced
      Paprika

Combine all ingredients, except water chestnuts and paprika, in a greased 1-1/2-quart casserole dish. Bake at 350° for 30 minutes. After about 15 minutes, cover top with water chestnuts and sprinkle with paprika. Yield: 4 servings.
    Variation: Cream of mushroom soup may be substituted for cream of chicken soup, and the top of the casserole may be covered with sliced mushrooms instead of water chestnuts.

CHICKEN-PAPRIKA CASSEROLE

    1 (10-3/4-ounce) can cream of
      mushroom soup
    1/4 cup milk
1-1/3 cups diced, cooked chicken
    1 teaspoon paprika
    1/2 teaspoon Worcestershire sauce
    14 salted crackers
      Butter or margarine
      Sliced mushrooms (optional)
      Pimiento (optional)

Combine soup and milk. Add chicken and seasonings. Pour into a greased 1-1/2-quart casserole dish. Cover with cracker crumbs and dot with butter. Bake at 350° for about 20 minutes. Garnish with sliced mushrooms and pimiento, if desired. Yield: 4 servings.

CHICKEN-GREEN NOODLE CASSEROLE

1 (3-1/2-pound) chicken
1 cup chopped green pepper
1 cup chopped onion
1 cup chopped celery
1/2 cup butter or margarine, melted
1/2 pound American cheese, cut into cubes
1 (6-ounce) can sliced mushrooms
1 (10-3/4-ounce) can cream of
   mushroom soup
1 (4-1/2-ounce) package green noodles
1 cup cheese crackers, crushed

Place chicken in a large saucepan. Cover with water and boil until chicken is done. Reserve stock. Cool chicken, remove meat from bones, and cut into bite-size pieces.

Sauté green pepper, onion, and celery in butter until tender. Add cheese and stir gently until cheese is melted. Add mushrooms and chicken, blending well, then stir in soup; mix well.

Boil noodles in chicken stock. Drain and combine with chicken mixture. Place in a greased 2-quart casserole dish, and top with crushed cheese crackers. Cool; seal and freeze. To serve, thaw and heat. Yield: 8 servings.

CHICKEN-NOODLE CASSEROLE

4 large chicken breasts
2 (10-3/4-ounce) cream of chicken soup
1/2 (10-3/4-ounce) can chicken broth
4 to 5 stalks celery, chopped
1/4 green pepper, chopped
1/4 medium onion, chopped
1 tablespoon butter or margarine
1 (4-ounce) can mushrooms with juice
8 green onion tops, cut into 1/2-inch pieces
3 tablespoons cooking sherry
1 (5-ounce) package noodles, cooked and
   drained
1/4 to 1/2 cup slivered almonds
   Buttered breadcrumbs
   Paprika

Cook chicken breasts; drain, cool, and cut into bite-size pieces. Heat soup and broth together and set aside. Cook celery, green pepper, and onion in butter until almost done. Combine soup, cooked vegetables, mushrooms, onion tops, and cooking sherry.

In a buttered 2-quart casserole dish, place a layer of cooked noodles and a layer of chopped chicken; cover with soup mixture and sprinkle with almonds. Repeat layers until all ingredients have been used. Cover top with buttered breadcrumbs and sprinkle with paprika. Bake at 350° for about 30 minutes, or until mixture bubbles. Yield: 8 servings.

CHICKEN SALONIKA

4 tablespoons olive oil or butter, divided
1/4 cup chopped onion
1/4 cup brown rice
1/2 cup sliced almonds
1 (3-pound) chicken, cut for frying
1/3 cup all-purpose flour
1 teaspoon salt
1/8 teaspoon pepper
1-1/2 cups milk
1/4 teaspoon thyme
   Pinch sugar
   Pinch cayenne pepper
3 tablespoons chopped pimiento
1-1/2 tablespoons cornstarch
1/2 cup half-and-half

Heat 2 tablespoons olive oil in a large heavy skillet. Add onion, rice, and almonds; sauté slowly, stirring occasionally, until golden brown. Remove from pan and spread over the bottom of a shallow 2-quart baking dish.

Put remaining 2 tablespoons olive oil in same pan and heat until sizzling. Dip pieces of chicken in mixture of flour, salt, and pepper. Fry quickly, just enough to brown chicken. Place chicken on top of rice.

Combine milk, thyme, sugar, cayenne pepper, and pimiento; pour over chicken and rice. Bake at 375° for 1 hour. Remove chicken from rice; keep warm. Mix cornstarch and half-and-half; add to rice mixture. Stir thoroughly and return to oven for 10 minutes. Serve chicken with rice. Yield: 4 to 6 servings.

CHICKEN-SHRIMP TETRAZZINI

2 whole chicken breasts
1 (5-ounce) package vermicelli
1 small onion, chopped
1 clove garlic, chopped
1/2 green pepper, chopped
1 cup chopped celery
1/4 cup butter or margarine
1 teaspoon chopped parsley
1 tablespoon Worcestershire sauce
1 (4-1/2-ounce) can shrimp
1 (10-3/4-ounce) can cream of
   mushroom soup
1 (8-ounce) can tomato sauce
   Shredded Cheddar cheese

Place chicken in a pan, cover with water, and cook until tender; cool. Remove meat from bones and cut into bite-size pieces. Cook vermicelli for half the time given in the package directions.

Sauté onion, garlic, green pepper, and celery in butter. Add parsley and Worcestershire sauce. Stir in chicken, vermicelli, shrimp, soup, and tomato sauce. Cool and spoon into a greased 2-1/2-quart casserole dish; seal and freeze. To serve, thaw in the refrigerator overnight. Top with shredded Cheddar cheese and bake at 325° for 45 minutes to 1 hour. Yield: 4 to 6 servings.

CHICKEN SPECIALTY CASSEROLE

    6 cups chopped cooked chicken
    1 (10-1/2-ounce) can chicken and rice soup
    1 (10-3/4-ounce) can cream of
      mushroom soup
    1 (6-ounce) can mushroom pieces, drained
    1 (8-1/2-ounce) can water chestnuts,
      drained and sliced
    1 (5-1/3-ounce) can evaporated milk
    1 (5-1/2-ounce) can chow mein noodles
    1 (4-ounce) can pimientos, chopped
      (optional)
1/2 pound sharp Cheddar cheese, shredded

Combine chicken, soups, mushrooms, water chestnuts, evaporated milk, chow mein noodles, and chopped pimientos. Taste and add additional seasonings if desired. Spoon into a greased 3-quart casserole dish and cover with shredded cheese. Bake, uncovered, at 350° for 30 minutes. Yield: 10 servings.

CHICKEN SUPREME

    1 (1-3/4- to 2-1/2-pound) fryer chicken
    2 teaspoons salt
      Pepper to taste
    1 medium onion, chopped
    1 cup uncooked regular rice
    3 cups chicken broth
    2 cups tomato juice

Simmer chicken, salt, and pepper in water to cover until tender. Remove chicken from broth, and reserve broth for later use. Remove skin from chicken; grind the skin. Remove meat from bones and cut into small pieces. Place chopped chicken and onion in a greased 3-quart casserole dish and cover with rice. Place ground skin over rice; pour 3 cups chicken broth and tomato juice over all. Bake at 350° for 30 minutes. Then increase heat to 400° for 15 minutes, or until brown. Yield: 8 servings.

CHICKEN-WILD RICE CASSEROLE

    2 (3-pound) whole fryer chickens
    1 cup water
    1 cup dry sherry
1-1/2 teaspoons salt
  1/2 teaspoon curry powder
    1 medium onion, sliced
  1/2 cup sliced celery
    1 pound fresh mushrooms
  1/4 cup butter or margarine
    2 (6-ounce) packages long-grain and wild
      rice with seasonings
    1 cup commercial sour cream
    1 (10-3/4-ounce) can cream of
      mushroom soup

Place chickens in a deep kettle; add water, sherry, salt, curry powder, onion, and celery. Cover and bring to a boil; reduce heat and simmer for 1 hour. Remove from heat; strain broth. Refrigerate chicken and broth at once, without cooling first.

When chicken is cool, remove meat from bones; discard skin. Cut meat into bite-size pieces. Rinse mushrooms and pat dry; slice and sauté in butter until golden, about 5 minutes, stirring constantly. (Reserve enough whole caps to garnish top of casserole; they may be sautéed along with sliced mushrooms.)

Measure chicken broth; use as part of the liquid for cooking rice, following directions for firm rice on the package. Combine chicken, mushrooms, and rice in a 3-1/2 - or 4-quart casserole dish. Blend in sour cream and mushroom soup and toss with the chicken and rice mixture. Arrange reserved mushroom caps in a circle over the top of the casserole. Cover; refrigerate overnight if desired. To heat, bake, covered, at 350° for 1 hour. The casserole may be completely prepared and frozen ahead of time. Yield: 8 to 10 servings.

CONTINENTAL CHICKEN CASSEROLE

3 tablespoons butter or margarine
6 tablespoons all-purpose flour
2 cups chicken broth
1 cup half-and-half
1 teaspoon prepared mustard
1/2 teaspoon salt
   Dash pepper
1/8 teaspoon allspice
1/8 teaspoon ground nutmeg
1/2 teaspoon sugar
1/8 teaspoon cayenne pepper
1/2 teaspoon paprika
1/2 teaspoon seasoned salt
1/4 cup dry sherry
4 hard-boiled eggs, cubed
4 cups cooked chicken, chopped
   Buttered breadcrumbs

Melt butter in a saucepan and stir in flour until smooth. Over low heat, slowly blend in broth, then half-and-half. Cook over medium heat until thick, stirring constantly. Combine all seasonings; then blend into sauce. Stir in sherry; fold in eggs and chicken. Turn into a buttered 3-quart casserole dish, top with crumbs, and bake at 350° for 30 minutes. (Leftover turkey may be substituted for chicken.) Yield: 10 to 12 servings.

CHICKEN TETRAZZINI

1 small chicken, cooked and boned (reserve broth)
1 (10-3/4-ounce) can cream of mushroom soup
1/4 pound shredded sharp cheese
1 teaspoon Worcestershire sauce
1/2 (10-3/4-ounce) can chicken broth
1 (2-1/2-ounce) can mushroom pieces, drained
1 teaspoon salt
1/2 (8-ounce) package spaghetti
   Toasted breadcrumbs

Cook chicken until tender enough to remove from bone. Cut into small pieces and place in a greased 2-quart casserole dish.

Heat mushroom soup, cheese, Worcestershire sauce, canned chicken broth, and broth from cooking chicken. Add mushroom pieces and salt.

Cook spaghetti in boiling salted water; drain, and place over chicken in a casserole dish. Pour sauce over all; top wth toasted breadcrumbs and bake at 300° for 15 to 20 minutes, or until bubbly. Yield: 6 servings.

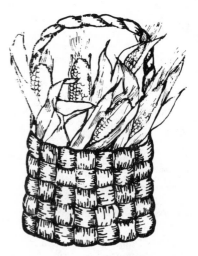

CURRIED CHICKEN-WILD RICE BAKE

1 (1-3/8-ounce) package dry onion soup mix
1 pint commercial sour cream
3 (2-1/2-pound) fryer chickens
2 cups dry sherry
1 cup water
1 teaspoon salt
   Dash pepper
1/2 teaspoon basil
   Pinch thyme
1 teaspoon curry powder
6 tablespoons minced fresh parsley
1 (10-3/4-ounce) can cream of mushroom soup
1-1/2 cups uncooked wild rice

Blend onion soup mix and sour cream in a bowl; allow to stand for 2 hours. Place chicken in a roasting pan; pour sherry and water over it; sprinkle with seasonings and parsley; cover roaster tightly. Bake at 300° for 1-1/2 hours, or until meat falls off the bones. Remove chicken from roaster, cover loosely, and set aside to cool.

Strain pan juices from roaster into saucepan and simmer until reduced to 1-1/2 cups. Blend in mushroom soup until smooth, and heat for a few minutes. (This is better if you blend by pouring liquid into canned soup.) Slowly combine with the sour cream mixture. The cream will not curdle if you blend slowly, pouring the hot liquid into cream mixture a little at a time.

Cook rice according to package directions. Skin and bone cooled chicken; cut into bite-size pieces. Combine with rice and turn into a buttered casserole dish. Pour sauce over and toss lightly. When ready to serve, heat, uncovered, at 350° for about 30 minutes. Excellent prepared

ahead of time; freezes beautifully. Yield:
12 servings.

ELEGANT CHICKEN CASSEROLE

    4 cups diced, cooked chicken
    4 cups chicken broth
1-1/2 cups diced celery
    1 cup diced American cheese
    1 large onion, diced
    2 eggs, beaten
    1 (10-3/4-ounce) can cream of
        mushroom soup
  1/2 teaspoon pepper
    2 teaspoons salt
    1 cup water chestnuts (optional)
    4 cups cracker crumbs, divided

Combine all ingredients except 1 cup cracker
crumbs saved to sprinkle on top of casserole.
Bake, uncovered, at 350° for 45 minutes. Yield:
8 to 10 servings.

HOT CHICKEN CASSEROLE

    2 cups chopped cooked chicken
    2 cups finely chopped celery
  1/2 cup chopped pecans or almonds
  1/2 cup chopped green pepper (optional)
  1/2 tablespoon chopped pimiento (optional)
    2 tablespoons minced onion
  1/2 to 1 tablespoon salt
    2 to 6 tablespoons freshly squeezed
        lemon juice
  3/4 cup mayonnaise
  1/2 cup shredded Cheddar cheese
    1 to 3 cups crushed potato chips

Combine all ingredients except cheese and
potato chips in a greased 3-quart casserole dish.
Top with cheese and potato chips. Bake at 350°
for 15 to 25 minutes, or until cheese is melted
and celery is tender. Yield: 4 to 6 servings.

HOT CHICKEN SALAD CASSEROLE

    2 cups diced cooked chicken
    2 cups diced celery
  1/2 cup slivered blanched almonds
  1/2 teaspoon salt
  1/2 teaspoon grated onion
    2 tablespoons freshly squeezed lemon juice
    1 cup mayonnaise
  1/2 cup shredded medium-sharp Cheddar
        cheese
  2/3 cup broken potato chips

Mix all ingredients except cheese and potato
chips; place in a shallow buttered casserole dish.

Combine cheese and potato chips and spread
over the top. Bake, uncovered, at 375° for 20
minutes. Yield: 6 servings.

EASY CHICKEN SOUFFLE

    3 tablespoons butter or margarine
    3 tablespoons all-purpose flour
    1 cup milk
      Pinch salt
    2 eggs yolks, well-beaten
1-1/3 cups boned, diced, cooked chicken
    1 teaspoon onion juice
    2 egg whites, well-beaten
  1/4 teaspoon cornstarch
  1/4 teaspoon sugar

Make a cream sauce of the butter, flour, milk,
and salt. Add beaten egg yolks, diced chicken,
and onion juice. When cool, add beaten egg
whites into which 1/4 teaspoon each of
cornstarch and sugar have been added when
half beaten. Place mixture into a greased 1-quart
casserole dish. Place in a pan of hot water and
bake at 325° for 1 hour. Yield: 6 servings.

HEN-IN-WINE CORNISH CASSEROLE

    1 tablespoon rosemary leaves
    1 cup dry white wine
    4 Rock Cornish hens, quartered
  1/4 cup all-purpose flour
    1 teaspoon salt
  1/2 teaspoon pepper
    1 teaspoon chopped fresh parsley
    1 clove garlic
  1/2 cup butter or margarine
    1 pound fresh mushrooms

Soak rosemary leaves in wine for 30 minutes
to 1 hour. Place pieces of hen in a paper bag
containing a mixture of flour, salt, pepper, and
parsley. Shake well to coat thoroughly. Brown
garlic clove in melted butter in a skillet and
remove. Add pieces of hen; brown quickly, and
remove to a casserole dish. Sauté mushrooms in
butter remaining in the skillet and add to the
casserole. Pour wine mixture over casserole, and
bake at 350° for 30 to 45 minutes. Yield:
4 servings.

Sage

Sage, one of the most popular of all
seasonings, should be used with a very light
touch because of its powerful flavor. It is a vital
ingredient in dressings and is particularly good
with mild-flavored meat dishes (pork, veal, or
poultry).

QUICK CHICKEN CASSEROLE

    1 (12-ounce) can chicken
    1 (3-ounce) can mushroom slices, drained
      and liquid reserved
    1 (2-ounce) jar pimientos, chopped
  1/4 cup finely minced onion
    1 tablespoon all-purpose flour
  1/4 cup mayonnaise
    3 tablespoons milk
    3 tablespoons mushroom liquid
  1/8 teaspoon salt
      Dash pepper
      Dash garlic salt
      Almond slivers
      Chow mein noodles, rice, or toast points

Cut chicken into pieces and place in a large bowl. Add drained mushroom slices, pimientos, and onion. Stir flour into mayonnaise. Mix milk and mushroom liquid and add seasonings to it. Blend mayonnaise and liquid into chicken; toss lightly. Place in a greased 1-1/2-quart casserole dish; top with almonds, and cover. Bake at 375° for 30 to 40 minutes. Serve with chow mein noodles, rice, or toast points. Yield: 6 servings.

Note: Almond slivers can be kept in a plastic bag in the freezer for about 6 months, then in the refrigerator for about 1 month.

HOT CHICKEN SALAD SURPRISE

    4 cups diced, cooked chicken
    2 (10-3/4-ounce) cans cream of
      chicken soup
    2 cups diced celery
    4 tablespoons minced onion
    2 cups slivered almonds
    1 cup mayonnaise
  3/4 cup chicken stock
    1 teaspoon salt
  1/2 teaspoon pepper
    4 tablespoons freshly squeezed lemon juice
    6 hard-cooked eggs, finely chopped
    1 cup cracker crumbs

Combine all ingredients except cracker crumbs and place in a greased 3- to 4-quart casserole dish. Cover with cracker crumbs. Bake at 350° for 40 minutes. Yield: 10 to 12 servings.

Parsley

Parsley is a mild-flavored herb that is as important for garnishing as it is for seasoning. Its flavor highlights meat and vegetable dishes. Parsley combines well with buttered breadcrumbs as a casserole topping.

PARTY CHICKEN CASSEROLE

    1 (3-1/2- to 5-pound) chicken, disjointed
    1 onion, sliced
    1 teaspoon salt
    1 bay leaf
    3 or 4 peppercorns
    1 (6-ounce) can sliced mushrooms, drained
      and liquid reserved
    1 cup evaporated milk, undiluted
  1/2 cup butter or margarine
  1/2 cup all-purpose flour
    1 teaspoon salt
  1/2 teaspoon turmeric
      Dash pepper
  1/4 teaspoon oregano
  1/2 cup shredded American cheese, divided
  1/2 cup slivered or whole blanched almonds
  1/2 cup slivered and toasted almonds

Cover chicken and onion with cold water in large saucepan. Add salt, bay leaf, and peppercorns; bring slowly to a boil. Reduce heat and simmer for 1 hour, or until chicken is tender. Cool chicken in broth; then remove skin and bones. Cut chicken into bite-size pieces. Strain and reserve broth.

Measure liquid from drained mushrooms; add enough chicken broth to make 3 cups. Add evaporated milk. Melt butter; blend in flour, 1 teaspoon salt, turmeric, and pepper. Add chicken broth mixture and cook over low heat, stirring constantly, until thickened. Add oregano and 1/4 cup cheese; stir until cheese melts. Add mushrooms, chicken, and 1/2 cup blanched almonds. Place into a greased 3-quart casserole dish, and sprinkle with toasted slivered almonds and remaining cheese. Bake at 350° until top is golden brown and sauce is bubbly. Yield: 6 to 8 servings.

TURKEY CASSEROLE

    2 tablespoons butter or margarine
    2 tablespoons all-purpose flour
    1 cup milk
  1/2 cup orange juice
    1 cup commercial sour cream
  1/4 cup sherry or fruit juice
    2 cups cooked rice
    2 oranges, peeled and sliced
    4 cups cooked, chopped turkey
  1/2 cup slivered almonds

Melt butter in a medium saucepan. Stir in flour and cook until smooth. Slowly add milk, a little at a time, and continue cooking until mixture is smooth and thick. Do not boil. Add orange juice and sour cream. Remove from heat. Stir in sherry.

Arrange rice in a greased 6-cup casserole dish; cover with a layer of orange slices. Add a layer of cooked turkey. Pour sauce over all and garnish with remaining orange slices. Sprinkle with almonds. Bake at 350° for 25 to 30 minutes. Yield: 6 servings.

TURKEY DIVAN

    1/3 cup butter or margarine
    1/3 cup all-purpose flour
      1 teaspoon salt
    1/8 teaspoon pepper
      2 cups milk
      1 cup shredded American cheese
    12 to 18 stalks fresh asparagus, cooked
      8 to 10 slices cooked turkey or chicken
      1 pimiento, cut into strips

Melt butter in a saucepan over low heat; blend in flour and seasonings. Add milk, stirring constantly, and cook until sauce is smooth and thickened. Add cheese and stir until melted. Arrange asparagus in a shallow baking dish, or in 6 individual casserole dishes. Pour half of the sauce over the asparagus. Arrange turkey or chicken over the sauce and cover with the remaining sauce. Garnish with pimiento strips. Bake at 375° for about 25 minutes, or until lightly browned. Yield: 6 servings.

TURKEY AND ALMOND CASSEROLE

    1/2 cup almonds, slivered
      2 tablespoons butter or margarine
      2 cups chopped cooked turkey
      1 (10-3/4-ounce) can cream of
        mushroom soup
      2 cups cooked rice
      1 cup milk
    1/2 teaspoon salt
    1/4 cup white wine
      1 cup buttered breadcrumbs

Brown almonds in butter. Combine with all other ingredients except breadcrumbs and place in a greased 1-1/2-quart casserole dish. Top with breadcrumbs; bake at 350° for 45 minutes.

Chicken or tuna may be substituted for the turkey. Yield: 6 servings.

INDIVIDUAL TURKEY CASSEROLES

    1/3 cup butter or margarine
    1/4 cup all-purpose flour
    1-1/2 teaspoons salt
    1/8 teaspoon pepper
    1-1/2 teaspoons curry powder
    1/2 teaspoon ground ginger
      3 cups milk
      1 tablespoon soy sauce
      1 (1-pound) can Chinese vegetables,
        drained
      2 cups turkey chunks
      2 cups cooked rice
      1 (3-ounce) can chow mein noodles

Melt butter in a saucepan. Blend in flour, salt, pepper, curry powder, and ginger. Add milk and soy sauce; cook, stirring constantly, until sauce is thickened and smooth. Fold in vegetables and turkey. Place an equal amount of rice in six 10-ounce individual casserole dishes; top each with an equal amount of the turkey mixture and noodles. Bake at 375° until hot and bubbly, about 15 minutes. Yield: 6 servings

QUICKIE TURKEY A LA KING

    1-1/2 cups cooked turkey (or chicken), cut into
        bite-size pieces
      1 (10-3/4-ounce) can cream of mushroom
        soup, undiluted
    1/2 teaspoon dried green onion
    1/4 teaspoon paprika
    1/4 teaspoon monosodium glutamate
    1/8 teaspoon white pepper
      1 tablespoon chopped parsley
      1 (2-ounce) jar pimientos, drained and
        finely chopped
      1 (4-ounce) can button or sliced
        mushrooms (optional)
      2 tablespoons sherry
        Melba toast, cornbread squares, or
        toasted English muffins
        Paprika
        Parsley sprigs (optional)

Place all ingredients except the last 4 in the top of a double boiler over rapidly boiling water. Cook for 10 to 12 minutes. Taste to see if salt is needed. Add sherry and remove from heat. Serve over melba toast, cornbread squares, or toasted English muffins. Sprinkle a little paprika over each serving and add a sprig of fresh parsley if desired. Yield: 6 to 8 servings.

FISH AND SHELLFISH CASSEROLES

CRAB DELIGHT

      1 pound crabmeat
    1/2 cup chopped celery
      2 tablespoons chopped green pepper
    1/4 cup melted butter or margarine
      2 tablespoons all-purpose flour
      1 cup milk
      1 egg yolk, beaten
      2 tablespoons freshly squeezed lemon juice
    1/2 teaspoon salt
    1/8 teaspoon pepper
      1 tablespoon melted butter or margarine
    1/4 cup dry breadcrumbs

Remove all shell or cartilage from crabmeat. Cook celery and green pepper in 1/4 cup melted butter until tender. Blend in flour. Add milk gradually and cook until thick, stirring constantly. Stir a little of the hot sauce into the egg yolk; add to remaining sauce, stirring constantly. Add lemon juice, seasonings, and crabmeat. Combine 1 tablespoon melted butter and breadcrumbs; sprinkle over casserole. Place in a well-greased 1-quart casserole dish. Bake at 350° for 20 to 25 minutes, or until brown. Yield: 6 servings.

CRABMEAT AU GRATIN

      3 tablespoons butter or margarine
    1/2 green pepper, minced
    1/2 onion, chopped
      3 tablespoons all-purpose flour
      2 cups milk
      2 cups boned crabmeat
    1/2 teaspoon salt
        Dash nutmeg
    1/2 cup shredded cheese
        Buttered breadcrumbs

Melt butter; add pepper and onion and cook for 5 minutes. Add flour, milk, crabmeat, salt, and nutmeg. Cook for 10 minutes. Pour into a shallow buttered baking dish, or use crab shells. Sprinkle with cheese and buttered breadcrumbs; bake at 350° until cheese is browned. Yield: 4 servings.

CRABMEAT SOUFFLE

      2 tablespoons butter or margarine
      2 tablespoons all-purpose flour
    3/4 teaspoon salt
    1/8 teaspoon pepper
      1 cup evaporated milk diluted with
        1 cup water
    1/2 cup soft breadcrumbs
      2 cups flaked cooked crabmeat
      3 egg yolks, well-beaten
      2 teaspoons minced parsley
      3 egg whites, stiffly beaten

Heat butter in a skillet; add flour, salt, and pepper, and mix well. Add milk gradually and bring to boiling point, stirring constantly. Add breadcrumbs and cook for 2 minutes longer. Remove from heat; add crabmeat, egg yolks, and parsley. Fold in stiffly beaten egg whites. Place in a greased 2-quart baking dish and bake, uncovered, at 350° for about 50 minutes. Yield: 6 servings.

CRABMEAT ST. JACQUES

    1/4 onion, chopped
    1/2 green pepper, chopped
    1/2 cup mushrooms, finely chopped
        Butter or margarine
      2 cups white sauce
        Salt and pepper
        Paprika
      1 teaspoon Worcestershire sauce
      1 pound crabmeat, canned
        Shredded American cheese
        Buttered breadcrumbs
        Paprika

Sauté onion, pepper, and mushrooms in a small amount of butter. Add the white sauce seasoned with salt, pepper, a generous amount of paprika, and Worcestershire sauce. Add crabmeat; stir to mix. Place mixture in a buttered casserole dish, and sprinkle top lightly with cheese, buttered breadcrumbs, and paprika. Bake at 450° for 15 minutes. Yield: 6 servings.

CRAB CASSEROLE

    2 (7-1/4-ounce) cans crabmeat, or 1 pound frozen crabmeat
    8 slices bread
1/2 cup mayonnaise
    1 cup chopped celery
    1 green pepper, chopped
    1 medium onion, chopped
1/2 teaspoon salt
    4 eggs, slightly beaten
    3 cups milk
    1 (10-3/4-ounce) can cream of mushroom soup
1/2 cup shredded Cheddar cheese

Drain and cut crabmeat into chunks. Dice half the bread into the bottom of a large buttered casserole dish. Combine crab, mayonnaise, celery, green pepper, onion, and salt. Spread over diced bread. Trim crusts from remaining bread, dice, and place over crab mixture. Mix eggs and milk together and pour over bread. Cover and refrigerate for several hours or overnight. Bake at 325° for 15 minutes. Remove from oven and spoon undiluted mushroom soup over top; sprinkle with shredded cheese. Return to oven and bake for 1 hour longer. Yield: 8 to 10 servings.

Note: For an additional touch of elegance, 1/2 cup slivered blanched almonds may be added to the mixture and/or a can of water chestnuts, drained and sliced, may be stirred in with the other vegetables.

CRABMEAT-ARTICHOKE CASSEROLE

    3 tablespoons butter or margarine
    3 tablespoons all-purpose flour
    1 teaspoon salt
1/8 teaspoon pepper
1/8 teaspoon dry mustard
1-1/2 cups milk
1/2 teaspoon Worcestershire sauce
       Dash hot pepper sauce
1/4 cup grated Parmesan cheese
    1 pound crabmeat
    1 (1-pound) can artichoke hearts, drained
    4 hard-cooked eggs, sliced
1/2 cup buttered breadcrumbs
1/4 cup grated Parmesan cheese

Melt butter; stir in flour, salt, pepper, and mustard until smooth. Gradually add milk and cook until thickened, stirring constantly. Add Worcestershire sauce, hot pepper sauce, 1/4 cup Parmesan cheese, and crabmeat; mix well. Arrange artichoke hearts in the bottom of a greased 1-1/2-quart casserole dish and cover with sliced eggs. Spoon in crab mixture. Top with buttered breadcrumbs which have been mixed with 1/4 cup Parmesan cheese. Bake at 350° for 30 to 40 minutes. Yield: 6 to 8 servings.

FISH PUDDING

    3 pounds bluefish, boned and skinned
1/2 teaspoon garlic salt
1/2 teaspoon pepper
1/2 teaspoon ground mace
1/2 cup butter or margarine
    1 tablespoon shortening
    1 (8-ounce) can tomato sauce
    1 medium onion, chopped
    1 green pepper, chopped
1/4 cup chopped celery
   12 salted crackers, crushed
    1 cup milk
    4 eggs, beaten

Grind, or finely chop the fish. Add garlic salt, pepper, and mace. Melt butter and shortening over medium heat; stir in tomato sauce. Add onion, pepper, and celery. Cook until onion is transparent; remove from heat. Stir in fish, crackers, milk, and eggs. Spoon into a 3-quart casserole dish. Cover and bake at 350° for 1 hour and 15 minutes. Yield: 8 servings.

LEMONFISH CASSEROLE

1-1/2 cups uncooked regular rice
  1 quart water
     Salt to taste
1/2 pound lemonfish steak
1/4 cup butter or margarine
     Tomato Sauce
     Orange slices
     Lemon wedges

Pour uncooked rice into the bottom of a large baking dish. Add water and salt. Cut lemonfish steaks into strips and lay strips across the rice. Add lumps of butter; cover and bake at 400° for 1 hour. Remove cover and brown top of fish for 5 to 10 minutes. To serve, pour Tomato Sauce over fish and rice. Garnish with fruits. Yield: 4 servings.

Tomato Sauce

  1 medium onion, chopped
1/4 cup butter or margarine
  3 (8-ounce) cans tomato sauce
  1 small green pepper, chopped
  1 tablespoon soy sauce
  3 drops hot pepper sauce
     Salt to taste
  2 cups water

Brown onion in butter. Add tomato sauce and other ingredients. Stir; cover. Bring mixture to a boil; reduce heat, and cook slowly for about 1-1/2 hours. Yield: about 3 cups.

OYSTERS "JOHNNY REB"

  2 quarts oysters, drained
1/2 cup finely chopped parsley
1/2 cup finely chopped shallots or onions
     Salt and pepper to taste
     Hot pepper sauce to taste
  1 tablespoon Worcestershire sauce
  2 tablespoons freshly squeezed lemon juice
1/2 cup melted butter or margarine
  2 cups fine cracker crumbs
     Paprika
3/4 cup half milk and half cream

Place a layer of oysters in the bottom of a greased shallow 2-quart baking dish. Sprinkle with half of the parsley, shallots, seasonings, lemon juice, butter, and crumbs. Repeat layers. Sprinkle with paprika. Just before baking, pour milk into evenly spaced holes, being very careful not to moisten crumb topping all over. Bake at 375° for about 30 minutes, or until firm. Yield: 12 to 15 servings.

CREOLE OYSTER PIE

  1 cup all-purpose flour
1/4 teaspoon salt
1/3 cup shortening
  1 tablespoon cold water
  1 quart oysters, drained
  1 cup all-purpose flour
  2 teaspoons salt, divided
1/4 teaspoon pepper
1/8 teaspoon ground mace
1/4 teaspoon paprika
  2 slices bacon, diced
  1 small onion, minced
  1 tablespoon minced green pepper
  8 to 10 drops hot pepper sauce
     Juice of 1 large lemon (about 2 tablespoons)
  1 tablespoon minced parsley
  2 tablespoons butter or margarine

In a large bowl, blend 1 cup flour, 1/4 teaspoon salt, shortening, and water. Roll to 1/4-inch thickness on a lightly floured board. Cut into 6 rounds, 2-3/4 inches in diameter, using a regular-size glass as a cutter. Then remove center of each round with 1-inch biscuit cutter. Set aside pastry rounds while preparing rest of recipe.

Dry the drained oysters on paper towels. Roll in a mixture of 1 cup flour, 1 teaspoon salt, pepper, mace, and paprika. Sauté bacon and onion until crisp and brown.

Place a layer of oysters close together in a buttered 10-1/2- x 6-1/2- x 2-inch baking dish. Sprinkle half of the bacon and onion mixture over oysters. Add half of the green pepper, the hot pepper sauce, 1 teaspoon salt, lemon juice, and parsley. Repeat layers. Dot with butter and place all the pastry rounds on top. Bake at 450° for 25 minutes, or until pastry rounds are golden. Serve at once. Yield: 6 servings.

OYSTERS CASINO

  3 slices bacon
  4 tablespoons chopped onion
  2 tablespoons chopped green pepper
  2 tablespoons chopped celery
  1 teaspoon freshly squeezed lemon juice
1/2 teaspoon salt
     Dash pepper
1/2 teaspoon Worcestershire sauce
  2 drops hot pepper sauce
  1 pint oysters, drained

Fry bacon; remove and crumble. Cook onion, green pepper, and celery in bacon drippings until tender. Add lemon juice, salt, pepper, Worcestershire sauce, and hot pepper sauce; mix well. Arrange drained oysters in a buttered baking dish. Spread bacon mixture over oysters. Bake at 350° for about 10 minutes, or until brown. Yield: 6 servings.

OYSTER CASSEROLE

    2 cups fine cracker crumbs
    1 tablespoon chopped pimiento
    1 teaspoon salt
1/4 teaspoon paprika
1/4 teaspoon celery salt
    2 teaspoons minced parsley
1/2 cup melted butter or margarine
    1 pint oysters
    1 egg, slightly beaten
2/3 cup cream of mushroom soup, undiluted

Combine cracker crumbs, pimiento, salt, paprika, celery salt, parsley, and melted butter; mix well. Line a greased shallow casserole dish with half the crumb mixture. Combine oysters, egg, and soup; pour this over the crumb mixture. Cover oysters with remaining crumb mixture. Bake at 350° for 1 hour. Yield: 8 servings.

OYSTER CREAM CASSEROLE

    2 cups oysters, drained
    1 cup soft breadcrumbs
    2 eggs, beaten
    1 cup commercial sour cream
    1 teaspoon salt
    1 tablespoon freshly squeezed lemon juice
    1 tablespoon chopped parsley
1/4 teaspoon pepper

Combine all ingredients and pour into a well-buttered 1-1/2-quart casserole dish. Bake at 350° for 35 to 40 minutes. Yield: 4 servings.

DEEP DISH OYSTER PIE

    Pastry for 2 piecrusts
    1 pint oysters, drained
    1 cup chopped celery
    1 teaspoon salt
1/2 teaspoon pepper
1/2 cup butter or margarine
    3 cups medium white sauce

Make pastry and line a shallow baking dish with half of it. Pick over oysters to remove any bits of shell. Place half of the oysters on the pastry, and half the celery, salt, pepper, butter, and white sauce. Then add a second layer of oysters and the other ingredients. Top with pastry. Bake at 375° for 45 minutes. Yield: 4 to 6 servings.

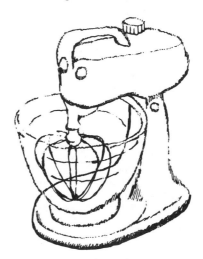

CORN AND OYSTER SCALLOP

    1 quart oysters, in liquor
    2 cups canned whole kernel corn, drained
1/4 large onion, minced
    Salt and pepper
1/4 teaspoon ground nutmeg
1/8 teaspoon ground mace
    3 cups cracker crumbs
1/4 cup oyster liquor
1/4 cup cream
3/4 cup dry Sauterne
1/2 cup butter or margarine
    Tartar sauce
    Lemon wedges

Drain oysters, reserving liquor; remove shell particles. Strain liquor and reserve. In mixing bowl, blend corn and onion; season with salt and pepper. Add nutmeg and mace; mix well.

Spread 1/3 of the crumbs in the bottom of a buttered 2-quart casserole dish. Cover the crumbs with the corn mixture; sprinkle with 1/3 of the crumbs. Arrange oysters over crumbs; sprinkle lightly with pepper, and top with remaining crumbs.

Blend oyster liquor, cream, and wine; pour over all. Dot generously with butter. Bake at 350° for 20 minutes, or until golden brown. Serve piping hot with tartar sauce and lemon wedges. Yield: 6 servings.

ESCALLOPED OYSTERS

- 1/2 cup butter or margarine
- 1/2 cup all-purpose flour
- 1/2 teaspoon salt
- 1/4 teaspoon pepper
- 1/2 teaspoon paprika
- 1 onion, minced
- 1/2 green pepper, minced
- 1 teaspoon freshly squeezed lemon juice
- 1 tablespoon Worcestershire sauce
- 1 quart oysters, in liquor
- 1/4 cup cracker crumbs

Melt butter; add flour and cook for 5 minutes, or until light brown. Add salt, pepper, and paprika, and cook for 3 minutes. Add minced onion and green pepper. Cook slowly for 5 minutes. Remove from heat. Add lemon juice, Worcestershire sauce, and oysters which have been heated in their own liquid. Pour into a greased baking dish and sprinkle with crumbs. Bake at 400° for 30 minutes. Yield: 8 to 10 servings.

SCALLOPED OYSTERS

- 1 pint oysters
- 2 cups cracker crumbs
- 1/2 teaspoon salt
  Dash pepper
- 1/2 cup melted butter or margarine
- 1/4 teaspoon Worcestershire sauce
- 1 cup milk

Drain oysters. Combine cracker crumbs, salt, pepper, and butter; sprinkle 1/3 of the crumb mixture into a buttered 1-quart casserole dish, and cover with a layer of oysters. Repeat layers, reserving a little of the crumb mixture for topping. Add Worcestershire sauce to milk; pour over casserole. Sprinkle remaining crumbs over top. Bake at 350° for 30 minutes, or until brown. Yield: 6 servings.

SEAFOOD-SPOONBREAD CASSEROLE

- 1 cup yellow cornmeal
- 2/3 teaspoon salt
- 1 cup water
- 1-1/2 cups milk, scalded
- 1/2 cup butter or margarine
- 1 egg, well-beaten
- 1/8 teaspoon pepper
- 2 cups oysters, drained (or shrimp, scallops, etc.)

Mix cornmeal, salt, and water; cook over low heat for about 15 minutes, stirring occasionally. Scald milk; add butter, and let melt; add to cornmeal mixture and stir until smooth. Slowly stir in beaten egg, pepper, and oysters; pour into a well-greased 1-1/2-quart casserole dish. Bake at 350° for 40 minutes. Yield: 4 servings.

SHERRIED LOBSTER

- 2 tablespoons butter or margarine
- 3 tablespoons all-purpose flour
- 1-1/2 cups milk, or 1 cup milk and 1/2 cup half-and-half
- 1 (2-ounce) jar pimientos, chopped
- 1/2 green pepper, finely chopped
- 1 cup tiny green peas
- 1/2 cup sherry
  Salt and pepper to taste
  Cubed meat from 1 large or 2 small boiled lobsters
  Shredded Romano cheese
  Paprika
  Toast squares

Melt the butter in the top of a double boiler and mix in flour. Add the next 6 ingredients and cook over boiling water to the consistency of a thick white sauce. Add lobster, place mixture in a 2-quart casserole dish. Sprinkle with shredded Romano cheese and paprika; bake at 400° until golden and bubbly. Serve on toast squares. Yield: 4 to 6 servings.

EASY SALMON CASSEROLE

- 2 tablespoons butter or margarine
- 1/2 teaspoon salt
  Dash pepper
- 1/2 teaspoon dry mustard
- 1 cup soft breadcrumbs
- 1/2 cup milk
- 2 eggs, slightly beaten
- 1 (1-pound) can flaked salmon, drained and liquid reserved

Melt butter. Add salt, pepper, and mustard; mix well. Add breadcrumbs and stir until butter mixture is absorbed. Add milk, eggs, and liquid from salmon. Add salmon and mix well. Pour into a well-greased 2-quart baking dish. Bake at 350° for 45 minutes, or until firm and brown. Yield: 6 servings.

SALMON CASSEROLE

   1 (5-ounce) package noodles
   1 (1-pound) can salmon
   1 (10-3/4-ounce) can cream of
     mushroom soup
1-1/4 cups milk
 1/4 cup chopped onion (optional)
 1/4 to 1/2 cup diced celery (optional)
   1 teaspoon salt
 1/8 teaspoon pepper
 1/2 cup buttered breadcrumbs
     Butter or margarine
     Paprika

Cook noodles in boiling salted water until tender. Drain, and rinse well with boiling water. Alternate layers of noodles and salmon in a greased 2-quart casserole dish. Combine soup, milk, onion, celery, salt, and pepper; pour over salmon and noodle mixture. Sprinkle breadcrumbs over top; dot with butter and sprinkle with paprika. Bake at 350° for about 30 minutes. Serve hot. Yield: 6 to 8 servings.

SALMON-NOODLE BAKE

   1 (8-ounce) package elbow macaroni
 1/2 cup minced onion
   2 tablespoons butter or margarine
   1 (10-3/4-ounce) can cream of celery soup
 2/3 cup milk
 1/2 pound sharp cheese, shredded
   1 teaspoon salt
     Dash pepper
 1/2 teaspoon dry mustard
   1 (1-pound) can salmon
   1 (10-ounce) package frozen green peas
   2 tablespoons grated Parmesan cheese

Cook macaroni according to package directions; drain. Sauté onion in butter; add soup, milk, cheese, and seasonings. Stir until cheese melts. Remove bones from salmon; thaw peas slightly to separate. Combine macaroni with sauce and add salmon and peas. Pour into a greased 2-quart casserole dish. Sprinkle with cheese and bake at 350° for 30 to 40 minutes. Yield: 6 servings.

SEA COAST DIABLE

   1 (27-ounce) can spinach or other greens,
     drained
 1/2 cup cream of celery soup
     Dash ground nutmeg
   2 (8-ounce) cans oysters, drained
   2 (4-1/2- to 6-1/2-ounce) cans shrimp,
     drained
   1 clove garlic, minced
 1/4 cup butter or margarine
 1/2 teaspoon Worcestershire sauce
     Dash hot pepper sauce
   2 tablespoons grated Parmesan cheese

Combine drained spinach, soup, and nutmeg. Line a greased shallow 1-1/2-quart baking dish with spinach mixture. Arrange drained oysters on spinach. Cover oysters with drained, rinsed shrimp. Sauté minced garlic in butter; add Worcestershire sauce and hot pepper sauce. Drizzle butter mixture over oysters and shrimp. Cover and bake at 350° for 35 minutes, or until heated through. Remove cover; sprinkle with Parmesan cheese and place under the broiler for several minutes to brown the cheese. Yield: 6 servings.

BERKLEY SEAFOOD CASSEROLE

   2 (10-ounce) cans frozen cream of shrimp
     soup, thawed
   2 (4-ounce) cans mushrooms, drained and
     liquid reserved
   2 tablespoons freshly squeezed lemon juice
   2 teaspoons soy sauce
   2 teaspoons celery salt
   1 cup shredded Swiss cheese and 1 cup
     grated Parmesan cheese, mixed
   1 pound crabmeat (fresh, frozen, or
     canned)
   2 pounds raw shrimp, boiled, shelled, and
     cleaned
   2 (8-ounce) packages fine noodles, cooked

Heat soup; add mushrooms, lemon juice, soy sauce, and celery salt. When thoroughly heated, stir in cheese, crabmeat, and shrimp. (Use mushroom liquid to thin mixture if it seems thick.) Spread cooked noodles in the bottom of a buttered casserole dish; pour hot mixture over noodles, place foil loosely over top, and bake at 375° for 25 to 30 minutes. Yield: 12 servings.

ROYAL SEAFOOD CASSEROLE

    2 (10-3/4-ounce) cans cream of
      shrimp soup
1/2 cup mayonnaise
    1 small onion, grated
3/4 cup milk
      Salt, white pepper, seasoned salt, ground
      nutmeg, and cayenne pepper
    3 pounds raw shrimp, cooked and cleaned
    1 (7-1/2-ounce) can crabmeat, drained
    1 (5-ounce) can water chestnuts, drained
      and sliced
1-1/2 cups diced celery
    3 tablespoons minced fresh parsley
1-1/3 cups uncooked white long-grain rice,
      cooked until dry and fluffy
      Paprika
      Slivered almonds

Blend soup into mayonnaise in a large bowl. Stir until smooth. Add onion; then milk. Now begin seasoning; use a heavy hand because the rice and the seafood are bland. When mixture is well seasoned, combine with other ingredients except paprika and almonds. Check seasonings; add a few tablespoons milk if mixture seems dry — it should be moist. Turn mixture into a large, shallow, buttered casserole dish; sprinkle with paprika and scatter almonds generously over the top. Bake, uncovered, at 350° for about 30 minutes, or until hot and bubbly. Freezes well. Yield: 10 servings.

CREOLE RICE AND SHRIMP

1-1/2 cups uncooked regular rice
    2 tablespoons shortening
    1 tablespoon all-purpose flour
    1 green pepper, chopped
    1 tablespoon minced onion
    1 clove garlic, chopped
    2 tablespoons tomato paste
    1 pinch cayenne pepper
    1 cup cooked shrimp
    1 cup water
      Salt and pepper to taste

Cook rice according to package directions. Heat shortening in a heavy skillet; add flour; cook and stir until light brown. This is a roux, the fat and flour foundation of most Creole dishes. Add green pepper, onion, garlic, tomato paste, and cayenne pepper. Add shrimp, water, salt, and pepper. Cook slowly for 1 hour. Place rice in a 2-quart casserole dish; add shrimp mixture. Cover and bake at 350° for 25 to 30 minutes. Yield: 4 servings.

JAMBALAYA CASSEROLE

    1 (5-ounce) package elbow spaghetti
    2 slices bacon, chopped
1/2 cup chopped onion
1/2 cup chopped green pepper
1/2 clove garlic, minced
    2 tablespoons all-purpose flour
2-1/4 cups canned tomatoes
1/2 pound cubed boiled ham
    1 cup cooked cleaned shrimp
1/4 cup breadcrumbs
    2 tablespoons grated Parmesan cheese
    2 tablespoons melted butter or margarine

Cook spaghetti according to package directions; drain and rinse. Brown chopped bacon in a skillet. Add onion, green pepper, and garlic, and brown. Stir in flour; add tomatoes and cook until thickened, stirring constantly. Add spaghetti, ham, and shrimp. Pour into a greased 1-1/2-quart casserole dish. Combine breadcrumbs, cheese, and butter; sprinkle over casserole. Bake at 350° for about 30 minutes. Yield: 4 servings.

SEAFOOD CASSEROLE

    1 (10-3/4-ounce) can cream of
      mushroom soup
1/3 cup salad dressing or mayonnaise
1/3 cup milk
    1 pound fresh, boiled, and deveined
      shrimp; or 1 (6-ounce) can, drained
    1 (5-ounce) can water chestnuts,
      drained and sliced
    1 cup diced celery
    2 tablespoons chopped parsley
    2 teaspoons grated onion
    2 cups cooked rice
      Dash hot pepper sauce
1-1/2 cups fresh breadcrumbs
    3 tablespoons melted butter or margarine

Combine soup, salad dressing, and milk in a greased 2-quart casserole dish. Mix in shrimp, water chestnuts, celery, parsley, onion, rice, and hot pepper sauce. Combine breadcrumbs and butter and sprinkle over the top. Bake at 350° for 30 minutes. Yield: 4 to 6 servings.

CURRIED SHRIMP AND RICE CASSEROLE

    1 tablespoon salt
    1 thick slice unpeeled lemon
    1 bay leaf
    4 pounds large raw shrimp
1-1/2 cups regular white long-grain rice
    1 tablespoon salt
      Sauce

Bring a large pot of water to a boil; add salt, lemon slice, and bay leaf. Add shrimp to rapidly boiling water and, after water returns to a boil, cook shrimp for 10 minutes; drain, shell, and devein. Refrigerate until needed.

To cook rice, bring water to a boil in a large saucepan which has a tight-fitting lid; add 1 tablespoon salt; stir in the rice and boil rapidly, uncovered, for 18 to 20 minutes. Start tasting at 18 minutes; rice may be done at that point — it must not be mushy. Drain rice; return to the hot saucepan; cover with several paper towels; then place the lid on tightly and return to the still warm eye on the stove, but with the heat turned off. Allow to stand until ready to use. (The paper towels will absorb all the moisture and rice will be dry.)

Sauce

    6 tablespoons butter or margarine
    3 tablespoons grated onion
    5 tablespoons all-purpose flour
    1 teaspoon curry powder
    3 cups warm milk or half-and-half
    1 teaspoon salt
      Dash white pepper
      Generous dash ground nutmeg
  1/4 cup dry sherry
    1 tablespoon minced parsley
      Paprika

Heat butter in a large saucepan and sauté onion until golden. Blend in flour and curry powder; cook for a few minutes, stirring constantly. Very slowly add warm milk, stirring constantly until thickened. Remove from heat; stir in salt, pepper, nutmeg, sherry, and parsley. Taste; add more seasonings if mixture is too bland.

Butter a large casserole dish. Starting with rice, arrange rice and shrimp in layers, pouring some of the sauce over each layer, ending with rice. Sprinkle with paprika, cover, and bake at 350° for 30 to 40 minutes. Yield: 12 to 15 servings.

Note: For added glamor, reserve about 8 shrimp; place over top of casserole and drizzle melted butter over them before baking the casserole.

CURRIED SHRIMP IN CASSEROLE

    5 pounds raw shrimp in the shell
    3 (10-3/4-ounce) cans cream of
      shrimp soup
    3 cups commercial sour cream
2-1/2 teaspoons curry powder
    1 medium onion, finely chopped
    2 tablespoons butter or margarine

Boil shrimp, shell, and devein. Combine soup, sour cream, curry powder, and cooked shrimp. Sauté onion in butter and add to the mixture. Allow mixture to stand for 1 to 2 hours before heating so the flavors will be well blended. When ready to serve, turn mixture into a large casserole dish; cover and bake at 325° until heated through, about 30 minutes. Serve over hot rice. Yield: 20 servings.

Note: This casserole may also be used to fill tiny pastry shells. Yield: 60 servings.

SHRIMP AND MUSHROOM CASSEROLE

1-1/2 tablespoons butter or margarine
    2 teaspoons chopped onion
    2 teaspoons chopped green pepper
    2 tablespoons all-purpose flour
  3/4 cup half-and-half
  1/4 teaspoon paprika
  1/2 teaspoon salt
  1/2 cup shredded cheese
    1 (6-ounce) can mushrooms, quartered
    1 pound shrimp, boiled and cleaned
      Buttered breadcrumbs

Melt butter; add onion and green pepper and cook until tender, but not brown. Add flour and blend. Add remaining ingredients, except breadcrumbs, and pour into a buttered casserole dish. Top with buttered breadcrumbs and bake at 350° for 20 minutes. Yield: 4 servings.

SHRIMP AND OLIVE CASSEROLE

- 3 tablespoons shortening
- 3 tablespoons all-purpose flour
  Pepper
- 1-1/2 cups milk
- 1/4 teaspoon Worcestershire sauce
- 1 cup diced celery
- 1-3/4 cups cooked or uncooked shelled shrimp
- 3/4 cup sliced stuffed olives
- 1 cup soft whole wheat breadcrumbs,
  or fresh bread cut into 1/4-inch cubes

Blend shortening, flour, and pepper. Gradually add milk, Worcestershire sauce, and celery; blend well. Cook for 10 minutes; add shrimp and cook for 3 minutes. Mix olives and breadcrumbs. Alternate layers of the shrimp mixture and the olive mixture in a greased 9- x 5- x 3-inch loafpan or a 2-quart casserole dish. Bake at 400° for 15 minutes. Yield: 4 to 6 servings.

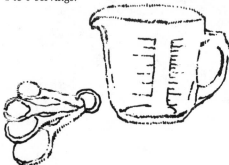

SHRIMP-BROCCOLI CRISP

- 1 cup cooked shrimp
- 1 (10-ounce) package frozen broccoli spears
- 1 (10-3/4-ounce) can cream of mushroom soup
- 1/4 cup milk or water
- 1/2 cup shredded American cheese
- 1 cup toasted breadcrumbs
- 2 tablespoons melted butter or margarine
- 2 hard-cooked eggs, sliced

Peel, devein, and cut shrimp in half. Cook broccoli according to package directions, just under tender. Heat soup and milk in a saucepan; stir until smooth. Stir in shrimp. Arrange layers of broccoli, soup mixture, and cheese in a greased baking dish. Sprinkle with crumbs and drizzle melted butter over the top. Bake at 350° for 20 minutes. Just before serving, slice hard-cooked eggs and arrange over casserole for garnish. Yield: 4 to 5 servings.

SHRIMP AND CORN AU GRATIN

- 1/4 (8-ounce) package medium noodles
- 1 (12-ounce) can whole kernel corn, drained and liquid reserved
- 1 (4-ounce) can mushrooms, chopped, drained, and liquid reserved
  About 1 cup milk
- 3 tablespoons butter or margarine
- 3 tablespoons all-purpose flour
- 1/2 teaspoon salt
- 3/4 cup shredded Cheddar cheese, divided
- 1 (5-ounce) can shrimp, deveined

Cook noodles according to package directions; drain and rinse. Drain liquid from corn and mushrooms into a measuring cup. Add enough milk to make 1-1/2 cups. Melt butter in a saucepan and stir in flour, mixing until smooth. Gradually add milk mixture, stirring constantly until thickened. Remove from heat and add salt and 1/2 cup cheese. Stir until cheese is melted. Place drained noodles in a pan; add corn, mushrooms, and shrimp. Pour cheese sauce over all and mix lightly with a fork. Turn into a well-greased 1-1/2-quart baking dish. Sprinkle remaining 1/4 cup cheese over top. Bake at 400° for 30 minutes. Yield: 6 servings.

SHRIMP CASSEROLE FOR A CROWD

- 1 green pepper, chopped
- 2 stalks celery, chopped
- 1 medium onion, chopped
- 2 cups water
  Small can pimientos, chopped
- 3 pounds cooked, deveined shrimp
- 1 (7-1/2-ounce) can crabmeat
- 4 hard-cooked eggs, thickly sliced
- 4 tablespoons butter or margarine
- 4 tablespoons all-purpose flour
- 2 cups half-and-half
- 1 cup shredded sharp Cheddar cheese
- 1/2 teaspoon salt
- 1/8 teaspoon pepper
- 3/4 cup buttered bread or cracker crumbs

Combine green pepper, celery, onion, and water; cook until vegetables are tender. Drain. Add pimiento, shrimp, crabmeat, and eggs.

To make cheese sauce, melt butter and stir in flour until smooth. Gradually add half-and-half and cook until mixture thickens, stirring constantly. Add cheese, salt, and pepper. Add sauce to shrimp mixture and place in a greased 3-quart casserole dish. Sprinkle crumbs over the top and bake at 400° for 15 minutes. Yield: 12 to 15 servings.

SHRIMP MEAL-IN-DISH

       1 pound shrimp, fresh or frozen
    1/2 cup butter or margarine
    1/2 cup thinly sliced onions
    1/3 cup all-purpose flour
    1/2 teaspoon salt
          Dash pepper
       3 cups milk
       1 cup cooked carrots
       1 cup cooked peas
       1 (8-ounce) can refrigerated biscuits

Shell and devein shrimp, and cut into chunks, reserving 3 whole shrimp for garnish. Melt butter in a large skillet or saucepan. Add onion and cook slowly until tender. Sprinkle with flour, salt, and pepper; gradually stir in milk over low heat. Cook, stirring constantly, until sauce thickens. Fold in carrots, peas, and shrimp. Pour into a greased 1-1/2-quart casserole dish. Arrange biscuits on top in a circle. Place 3 shrimp in the center of the circle. Bake at 450° for 12 to 15 minutes, or until biscuits are well-browned and shrimp are pink. Yield: 6 servings.

SHRIMP PILAFF

       2 tablespoons chopped green pepper
    1/4 cup chopped celery
       2 tablespoons minced onion
    1/2 cup uncooked regular rice
    1-1/2 tablespoons salad oil
    1/2 cup water
       1 cup canned tomatoes
       1 teaspoon salt
       1 to 2 teaspoons chili-pepper mix
       2 cups shrimp, canned or cooked

Cook green pepper, celery, onion, and rice together in salad oil over low heat until rice is browned. Stir in water and tomatoes. Season with salt and chili-pepper mix. Add shrimp and spoon into a greased 2-quart casserole dish; bake at 350° until rice is fluffy and tender. Yield: 4 servings.

SHRIMP DELISH

    1/2 cup celery soup
    1/4 cup milk
       1 heaping tablespoon grated onion
    1/2 small green pepper, finely chopped
       1 tablespoon Worcestershire sauce
          Dash cayenne pepper
    1/4 teaspoon salt
          Pepper to taste
       1 tablespoon freshly squeezed lemon juice
       1 tablespoon sherry
       1 to 1-1/2 cups boiled small shrimp
          Mayonnaise
          Cracker crumbs
          Grated Parmesan cheese
          Paprika

Combine soup, milk, onion, green pepper, Worcestershire sauce, cayenne pepper, salt, pepper, lemon juice, and sherry. Add shrimp to the mixture and place in a greased 1-1/2-quart casserole dish. Coat the top with mayonnaise. Sprinkle top with cracker crumbs, Parmesan cheese, and paprika. Bake at 325° for 40 minutes, or until bubbly. Yield: 4 servings.

SHRIMP DINNER CASSEROLE

       1 cup diced celery
    1-1/2 cups chopped green onions with tops
       3 cloves garlic, minced
    1/3 cup butter or margarine
       1 (10-3/4-ounce) can cream of
          mushroom soup
    1/2 cup water
       3 tablespoons minced parsley
       3 cups cooked rice
       2 slices bread, moistened
       1 teaspoon salt
    1/4 teaspoon pepper
       1 pound peeled and deveined shrimp,
          halved
    3/4 cup buttered breadcrumbs

Cook celery, onion, and garlic in butter until tender. Add soup, water, parsley, rice, and bread. Cook for about 10 minutes. Add seasonings and shrimp. Pour into a greased 2-1/2-quart casserole dish. Top with buttered breadcrumbs. Bake at 375° for 30 minutes. Yield: 6 servings.

Basil

Basil's aromatic flavor is especially popular in dishes with a tomato base. It is a favorable addition to seafood, beef, veal, pork, lamb, and vegetable casseroles.

BAKED TROUT AND CHEESE

   1 pound trout fillets
   6 ounces American cheese, sliced
   1/4 cup chopped parsley
   1 teaspoon ground oregano or thyme
   1/4 cup salad oil
   2 medium onions, chopped
   2 tablespoons all-purpose flour
   1/8 teaspoon salt
   1/8 teaspoon pepper
   1-1/2 cups milk

Alternate layers of fish and cheese in a lightly greased shallow baking dish, ending with cheese. Sprinkle with parsley and oregano. Heat salad oil in a skillet; add onions and cook until tender, stirring frequently. Mix in flour, salt, and pepper. Add milk; cook, stirring constantly, until thickened. Pour over fish. Bake at 400° for about 20 to 30 minutes, or until fish flakes easily with a fork. Yield: 4 servings.

CREAMY TUNA-RICE CASSEROLE

   1 medium onion, chopped
   2 (7-ounce) cans tuna,
      drained and liquid reserved
   1-1/2 cups cooked rice
   1 (10-3/4-ounce) can cream of
      celery soup
   1 cup half-and-half
   1 teaspoon poultry seasoning
   1/4 cup diced pimiento
   1 (1-pound) can peas, drained

Cook onion in oil drained from tuna. When onion is tender, add rice, soup, half-and-half, poultry seasoning, and pimiento; mix well. Gently mix in peas and tuna which has been broken into chunks; pour into a greased casserole dish. Bake at 375° for about 40 minutes. Yield: 6 servings.

CRUNCHY TUNA BAKE

   1 (5-ounce) can chow mein noodles
   1 (7-ounce) can tuna
   1 cup salted mixed nuts, chopped
   1 cup chopped celery
   1/4 cup chopped onion
   1 (10-3/4-ounce) can cream of
      mushroom soup
   1/4 cup milk
   1 (2-ounce) jar pimientos, chopped
      Salt and pepper to taste

Mix all ingredients together well. Place in a greased 1-1/2-quart baking dish. Sprinkle a few chow mein noodles over top. Bake at 375° for 30 minutes. Yield: 6 servings.

SHRIMP THERMIDOR

   3/4 pound cooked, peeled, cleaned shrimp
   1 (4-ounce) can mushroom stems
      and pieces, drained
   1/4 cup butter or margarine, melted
   1/4 cup all-purpose flour
   1 teaspoon Worcestershire sauce
   1/2 teaspoon dry mustard
   1/4 teaspoon salt
      Dash cayenne pepper
   2 cups milk
   1/2 cup pitted ripe olives,
      sliced crosswise
      Grated Parmesan cheese
      Paprika

Cut large shrimp in half. Sauté mushrooms in butter for 5 minutes. Blend in flour, Worcestershire sauce, and seasonings. Add milk gradually and cook until thick, stirring constantly. Add olives and shrimp. Place into 6 well-greased, individual shells or six greased 5-ounce custard cups. Sprinkle with cheese and paprika. Bake at 400° for 10 to 15 minutes, or until cheese is browned. Yield: 6 servings.

SPAGHETTI-SHRIMP RING

   1 (8-ounce) package spaghetti
   2 tablespoons chopped green pepper
   2 tablespoons chopped onion
   2 tablespoons butter or margarine
   1 cup tomato puree
   3 eggs, beaten
      Salt and pepper
   1 teaspoon Worcestershire sauce
   1/2 pound American cheese, shredded
   1-1/2 cups cooked shrimp
   1-1/2 cups cooked peas
   4 tablespoons butter or margarine

Cook broken spaghetti according to package directions; drain. Cook green pepper and onion in butter. Add tomato puree, eggs, seasonings, Worcestershire sauce, cheese, and spaghetti. Spoon into a buttered ring mold. Bake at 325° for 50 minutes. Unmold, and fill center with the shrimp and peas heated in butter. Yield: 8 to 10 servings.

Turmeric
   Turmeric, a member of the ginger family, is vivid yellow in color and faintly bitter in taste. Turmeric gives a pleasant flavor to fish and seafood dishes.

SHRIMP-RICE CASSEROLE

1-1/4 pounds shrimp
1/2 large onion, chopped
  1 tablespoon butter or margarine
  1 (10-3/4-ounce) can cream of
    mushroom soup
1/2 tablespoon freshly squeezed lemon juice
    Dash garlic salt
    Salt and pepper to taste
3/4 cup cooked rice
1/2 cup commercial sour cream
3/4 cup shredded cheese
1/2 green pepper, sliced

Cook and clean shrimp. Sauté onion in butter until tender. Make a sauce by adding soup, lemon juice, and seasonings. Fold rice and shrimp into the sauce. Fold in sour cream and pour into a greased 1-quart baking dish. Sprinkle shredded cheese on top and garnish with green pepper rings, parboiled for 2 minutes. Bake at 325° for 30 minutes. Yield: 6 servings.

TUNA BAKE

1/4 cup milk
  1 (7-ounce) can tuna
  1 teaspoon Worcestershire sauce
  2 teaspoons chopped onion
  2 hard-cooked eggs, chopped
1/2 cup chopped ripe olives
  1 cup cooked rice
  1 (10-3/4-ounce) can cream of
    mushroom soup
1/4 teaspoon paprika
  1 cup crushed potato chips

Combine first 8 ingredients and mix well. Spoon into a greased 2-quart casserole dish. Sprinkle top with paprika; spread crushed potato chips on top. Bake at 350° for 25 to 30 minutes. Yield: 6 to 8 servings.

TUNA-BROCCOLI ALMONDINE

  2 (10-ounce) packages frozen broccoli,
    or 1-1/4 pounds fresh broccoli
  2 (7-ounce) cans tuna, drained and flaked
1/2 cup slivered almonds
1/4 cup butter or margarine
1/4 cup all-purpose flour
1/2 teaspoon salt
1/8 teaspoon pepper
    Dash ground nutmeg
  2 cups milk
  1 tablespoon cooking sherry
    Paprika

Cook broccoli until tender; drain and arrange in a buttered 1-1/2-quart casserole dish. Spread tuna evenly over broccoli. Sauté almonds in butter until lightly browned; remove from butter and drain on paper towels.

Blend flour, salt, pepper, and nutmeg into butter. Add milk and cook over low heat, stirring constantly, until sauce is smooth and thickened. Stir sherry into sauce and pour over tuna. Sprinkle with paprika. Bake at 350° for 25 minutes, or until bubbly. Sprinkle browned almonds over top just before serving. Yield: 6 servings.

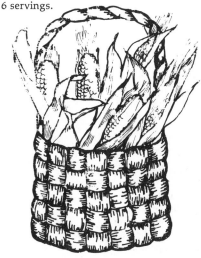

TUNA AU GRATIN

  3 tablespoons butter or margarine, divided
1/3 cup minced green pepper
  3 tablespoons minced onion
  2 tablespoons all-purpose flour
  1 cup milk
  1 (7-ounce) can tuna, drained
1/2 teaspoon salt
1/8 teaspoon pepper
1/2 teaspoon Worcestershire sauce
1-1/2 tablespoons chopped pimiento

Melt 1 tablespoon butter in a heavy skillet over low heat. Add green pepper and onion; sauté for 5 minutes. Melt 2 tablespoons butter in a saucepan over low heat; add flour and blend. Add milk; cook until thick, stirring constantly. Break tuna into large chunks. Add salt, pepper, Worcestershire sauce, pimiento, tuna, and sautéed green pepper and onion. Pour into 4 greased individual casserole dishes. Bake at 375° for 15 minutes, or until bubbly. Serve hot. Yield: 4 servings.

DEVILED TUNA CASSEROLE

    2 (7-ounce) cans tuna
    1 tablespoon grated onion
    1 tablespoon freshly squeezed lemon juice
    2 tablespoons chopped parsley
    1/2 teaspoon garlic salt
    1/4 cup butter or margarine
    1/4 cup all-purpose flour
    1/2 teaspoon salt
        Dash cayenne pepper
    2 cups milk
    1 cup soft bread cubes
    1/2 cup crushed potato chips

Drain tuna; break into large pieces. Add onion, lemon juice, parsley, and garlic salt. Melt butter; blend in flour, salt, and pepper. Add milk gradually and cook until thick and smooth, stirring constantly. Fold in bread cubes and tuna mixture. Place in a well-greased 1-quart casserole dish; cover with potato chips and bake at 400° for 15 to 20 minutes. Yield: 6 servings.

DOODLE-NOODLE CASSEROLE

    1 (5-ounce) package noodles
    1 (7-ounce) can tuna, drained
    1/2 cup mayonnaise
    1 cup chopped celery
    1/2 cup chopped onion
    1/4 cup chopped green pepper
    1/4 cup chopped pimiento
    1 teaspoon salt
    1 (10-3/4 ounce) can cream of celery soup
    1 cup milk
    1 cup sharp shredded cheese
    1/2 cup slivered, blanched, toasted almonds

Cook noodles according to package directions; drain. Combine noodles and tuna; add mayonnaise, vegetables, and salt. Blend in soup and milk; stir well. Heat on top of range and add cheese. Stir until cheese melts. Spoon into a greased 1-1/2-quart casserole dish; top with almonds. Bake at 425° for 20 minutes. Yield: 8 servings.

Dill

Dill should be used with a light touch and added near the end of cooking time. Its unique flavor is particularly good in beef, fish, and vegetable dishes.

TUNA-CASHEW CASSEROLE

    1 (3-ounce) can chow mein noodles
    1 (10-3/4-ounce) can cream of mushroom
        soup, undiluted
    1/4 cup water
    1 (7-ounce) can chunk-style tuna
    1 (6-ounce) can cashew nuts
    1 cup finely diced celery
    1/4 cup minced onion
        Pepper

Set aside half of the noodles. In a greased 1-1/2-quart casserole dish, combine the remaining noodles, mushroom soup, water, tuna, cashew nuts, celery, onion, and pepper. Taste and add salt if necessary. Sprinkle remaining noodles over top and bake at 325° for 40 minutes. Yield: 4 servings.

TUNA-NOODLE CRISP

    1 (5-ounce) package noodles
    1/4 cup shortening
    1/3 cup chopped onion
    2 tablespoons chopped green pepper
    1 (11-ounce) can Cheddar cheese soup
    1/2 cup milk
    1 tablespoon chopped pimiento (optional)
    1 teaspoon salt
    1/8 teaspoon pepper
    1 (7-ounce) can tuna
    1/2 cup breadcrumbs

Cook noodles in boiling salted water according to package directions; drain. Melt shortening in a large skillet; add onion and green pepper and cook until tender. Stir in soup, milk, pimiento, salt, and pepper; bring to a boil. Add cooked noodles and tuna. Place mixture in a greased 1-1/2- or 2-quart casserole dish. Sprinkle breadcrumbs on top. Bake at 350° for 25 to 30 minutes. Yield: 4 to 6 servings.

Note: To freeze, leave off breadcrumbs, cover tightly, and freeze. Thaw overnight. The next day bake as directed above.

TUNA-CORN CASSEROLE

2 (7-ounce) cans tuna
1/4 cup finely chopped onion
1 tablespoon all-purpose flour
1 cup evaporated milk
1 (12-ounce) can whole kernel corn
1 (3- or 4-ounce) can sliced mushrooms,
including liquid
1 tablespoon freshly squeezed lemon juice
1 teaspoon Worcestershire sauce
1/4 cup chopped ripe olives
1 (4-ounce) can julienne potato sticks

Drain oil from tuna into a saucepan. Add onion and cook until tender but not brown. Blend in flour. Stir in evaporated milk, corn, and mushrooms with liquid; bring to a boil. Remove from heat; stir in remaining ingredients except potato sticks. Place in a greased 2-quart casserole dish; arrange potato sticks around edge. Bake at 375° for 25 minutes. Yield: 4 to 6 servings.

TUNA-LIMA BEAN CASSEROLE

1 (10-ounce) package frozen lima beans
1-1/2 cups cooked macaroni
1/2 cup chopped onion
2 tablespoons butter or margarine
1 cup milk
1 (10-3/4-ounce) can cream of celery soup
1 (7-ounce) can tuna, drained
2 pimientos, chopped
1 tablespoon freshly squeezed lemon juice
1/2 cup buttered bread or cracker crumbs

Cook lima beans according to package directions; drain. Cook macaroni in boiling salted water until tender; drain. Sauté onion in butter until softened in a medium-size heavy saucepan; stir in milk and soup; heat slowly, stirring often. Stir in tuna, lima beans, pimientos, and lemon juice; simmer for 10 minutes. Fold in cooked macaroni. Pour into a greased 1-1/2-quart casserole dish. Sprinkle crumbs on top. Bake at 350° for 20 minutes, or until bubbly. Yield: 6 servings.

TUNA CASSEROLE

3 cups hot cooked rice
1 cup flaked tuna
1/2 cup sliced stuffed olives
2 hard-cooked eggs, sliced
1/4 teaspoon salt
Dash pepper
1 cup salad dressing or mayonnaise
1/2 cup milk

Divide rice, reserving 1 cup for topping. Save 5 slices stuffed olive and 3 slices hard-cooked eggs for garnish.

·Place alternate layers of rice, tuna, olives, and eggs in a greased 1-3/4-quart casserole dish. Place in a pan of hot water and bake, covered, at 400° for about 15 minutes. Add salt and pepper to salad dressing. Gradually add milk, stirring until smooth. Pour over contents of casserole. Top with the reserved 1 cup cooked rice. Bake, uncovered, for about 15 minutes longer; do not overcook. If overcooked, sauce will curdle. Serve hot. Yield: 6 to 8 servings.

Note: All of the rice may be used in the layers and buttered breadcrumbs may be used for a topping.

TUNA-WATER CHESTNUT CASSEROLE

1/2 cup regular rice, cooked dry and fluffy
1 (6-ounce) can water chestnuts,
drained and sliced
2 stalks celery, diced
1/2 green pepper, diced
1 tablespoon dried minced onion
1 (10-3/4-ounce) can cream of
mushroom soup
2 tablespoons freshly squeezed lemon juice
1/2 teaspoon salt
1 teaspoon Worcestershire sauce
1 teaspoon soy sauce
1 (7-ounce) can tuna, drained
Paprika

Cook rice according to package directions. While rice boils, combine all ingredients except tuna and paprika. Lightly stir in rice, then flaked tuna. Turn into a greased shallow 2-quart casserole dish, and sprinkle with paprika. Cover and bake at 350° for 25 minutes. Yield: 4 to 5 servings.

MEATLESS CASSEROLES

BARLEY CASSEROLE

1/2 cup butter or margarine
1 cup quick-cooking, fine pearl barley
1 medium onion, chopped
1/2 cup slivered almonds
1 (2-ounce) package dehydrated onion soup
2 cups chicken broth
1 (3-ounce) can mushroom slices, drained and liquid reserved, or 3/4 to 1 cup fresh mushrooms
1 (5-ounce) can water chestnuts, drained and sliced

Heat butter in a saucepan; add barley and onion and sauté only until a light golden color. Add almonds, dry onion soup, and chicken broth. Sauté mushrooms for a few minutes in a little butter; add to barley along with water chestnuts and liquid drained from the canned mushrooms. Stir well; turn into a greased casserole dish; cover and bake at 350° for 1 hour, adding more liquid if necessary. (A little more chicken broth may be used if required.)

This casserole may be prepared a day or two ahead of time and refrigerated before baking; leftovers freeze well. Yield: 6 servings.

GRITS CASSEROLE

1 cup regular grits
3 cups boiling water
1/2 teaspoon salt
1/4 cup butter or margarine
4 eggs, beaten
1 cup milk
1/4 cup shredded Cheddar cheese

Pour the grits into boiling salted water. Mix well and cook until thickened. Add butter, eggs, milk, and cheese. Stir thoroughly and place into a greased 2-quart casserole dish. Bake at 350° for about 30 minutes. Yield: 4 to 6 servings.

GRITS SOUFFLE

5 cups cold water
1 cup uncooked regular grits
1/2 cup butter or margarine, softened
2 eggs, beaten
1/2 teaspoon cayenne pepper
Dash salt
Dash hot pepper sauce
1/2 pound sharp Cheddar cheese, shredded

Bring water to a boil in a large saucepan; add grits and cook until mixture thickens. Add other ingredients and mix well. Spoon mixture into a greased 2-quart casserole dish. Bake at 350° for 1 hour. This may be prepared ahead of time and refrigerated until time to bake. Yield: 8 servings.

BAKED CHEESE GRITS

1-1/2 cups regular grits
6 cups boiling salted water
1/2 cup butter or margarine
1 (6-ounce) roll garlic cheese
3 tablespoons cooking sherry
3 tablespoons Worcestershire sauce
1/2 teaspoon hot pepper sauce
3 eggs, beaten

Cook grits in boiling salted water for about 2 or 3 minutes. Blend in butter, cheese, sherry, and sauces; stir in beaten eggs and mix well. Spoon mixture into a greased 2-quart baking dish and bake at 300° for about 1 hour. Serve hot. Yield: 6 to 8 servings.

CHEESE GRITS CASSEROLE

    2 cups boiling water
    1 teaspoon salt
    1 cup instant grits
    2 cups whole milk
1/4 cup butter or margarine
    4 ounces sharp Cheddar cheese, shredded
      Paprika

Pour boiling water into a large saucepan. Add salt and grits; stir well. Add milk and butter; mix well. Spoon into a buttered 3-quart casserole dish; sprinkle shredded cheese on top. Bake at 350° for 20 to 30 minutes, or until mixture thickens. Remove from oven and sprinkle generously with paprika. Serve hot. Yield: 8 servings.

SOUTHERN GRITS CASSEROLE

1-1/2 cups grits
    4 cups boiling water
1-1/2 teaspoons salt
1/2 teaspoon grated orange rind
    6 tablespoons butter or margarine
1-1/2 cups orange juice
    5 eggs, slightly beaten
      Orange slices
      Sugar

Pour grits into boiling water; add salt and orange rind. Stir grits constantly until mixture is thickened but not dry. Remove from heat; add butter and orange juice, stirring until well blended. Gently stir in eggs. Spoon into a greased 2-1/2-quart casserole dish and bake at 350° for 55 minutes, or until knife comes out clean when inserted 1 inch from the middle of the casserole. Garnish with fresh orange slices and sprinkle with sugar. Yield: 6 to 8 servings.

GREEN RICE

3/4 cup shredded cheese
    6 tablespoons minced parsley
1/4 teaspoon salt
    2 tablespoons chopped onion
    3 tablespoons melted butter or margarine
2-1/4 cups cooked rice
3/4 cup milk
    1 egg, beaten

Combine cheese, parsley, salt, onion, butter, and rice. Combine milk and egg; add to rice mixture. Blend thoroughly; turn into an oiled ring mold or a 2-quart baking dish. Cover and bake at 350° for 1 hour. Yield: 6 servings.

EASY RICE CASSEROLE

1/4 cup butter or margarine
    1 medium onion, chopped
    1 cup uncooked regular rice
    1 (10-1/2-ounce) can consommé
    1 (10-1/2-ounce) can beef bouillon

Melt butter in a skillet; add onion and sauté. In a greased 1-1/2-quart casserole dish, add uncooked rice. Over this pour the consommé and bouillon; stir in onion and butter. Bake, covered, at 350° for about 30 minutes or longer. Uncover during the last few minutes for rice to brown. Yield: 4 to 6 servings.

ITALIAN RICE CASSEROLE

    1 cup chopped onion
1/2 cup chopped green pepper
1/2 cup chopped celery
    1 tablespoon salad oil
    1 pound ground beef
    1 (18-ounce) can tomatoes
    1 (6-ounce) can Italian tomato paste
    1 (2-ounce) can mushroom pieces
    2 tablespoons chopped parsley
    1 teaspoon salt
1/2 teaspoon thyme
1/2 teaspoon pepper
1/4 teaspoon marjoram
    1 cup uncooked regular rice
    1 cup shredded Cheddar cheese

Sauté onion, green pepper, and celery in salad oil until almost transparent. Add ground beef and cook until browned. Add tomatoes, tomato paste, mushroom pieces, parsley, and seasonings. Simmer for 1 hour over low heat.

Meanwhile, cook rice in boiling salted water according to package directions. Mix rice with sauce and place in a shallow baking dish. Top with shredded cheese and bake at 350° for 15 to 20 minutes. Yield: 6 servings.

OLIVE-RICE CASSEROLE

    1 cup uncooked regular rice
    1 cup diced Cheddar cheese
    1 (3-ounce) jar sliced stuffed olives
    1 cup drained tomatoes
1/2 cup chopped onion
1/2 cup salad oil
    1 cup water
      Salt and pepper to taste

Combine all ingredients in a greased 2-quart baking dish. Bake, uncovered, at 350° for 1 hour. Yield: 4 to 6 servings.

MEXICAN RICE CASSEROLE

    4 slices bacon
  1/2 cup chopped onion
  1/2 cup chopped green pepper
    1 cup uncooked regular rice
    1 pound ground beef
    1 small clove garlic
1-3/4 cups water
    1 (8-ounce) can tomato sauce
  3/4 cup raisins
    2 teaspoons salt
    1 tablespoon chili powder
2-1/2 cups shredded cheese

Fry bacon until crisp. Remove from pan, drain, and crumble. Add onion and pepper to the bacon drippings and cook until tender. Add rice and cook until golden. Stir in beef and garlic; cook until meat is almost done. Stir in water, tomato sauce, raisins, and seasonings. Heat to boiling. Reduce heat, cover, and simmer for 20 minutes. Spoon half of the mixture into a greased 2-quart casserole dish. Sprinkle with half of the cheese and half of the crumbled bacon. Add remainder of meat mixture and top with remaining cheese and bacon. Bake at 450° for about 15 minutes, or until cheese is bubbly. Yield: 8 servings.

RICE CASSEROLE

  1/2 cup butter or margarine, melted
    1 cup uncooked regular rice
    1 (10-1/2-ounce) can beef consommé
    1 (10-1/2-ounce) can onion soup
    2 tablespoons Worcestershire sauce
  1/8 to 1/4 teaspoon cayenne pepper
       (optional)

Combine butter and rice in a skillet; cook over low heat until rice is lightly browned. Pour into a greased 2-quart baking dish. Add remaining ingredients. Stir lightly with a fork. Cover and bake at 350° for 1 hour. (Do not stir while baking.) Yield: 6 to 8 servings.

RICE-SOUR CREAM CASSEROLE

  3/4 pound sharp Cheddar cheese
    2 cups commercial sour cream
    1 (4-ounce) can green chile peppers,
       drained and chopped
    1 (4-ounce) can sweet red peppers, drained
       and chopped, or 1 small jar pimiento
       strips, drained
4-1/2 cups cooked rice
       Salt and pepper

Reserve a piece of the cheese to shred for topping (the size depends on size of casserole); cut remainder into strips. Combine sour cream and green and red peppers. Season the rice with salt and pepper. In a buttered shallow 1-1/2-quart casserole dish, arrange layers of rice, sour cream mixture, and cheese strips, ending with rice. Sprinkle with the reserved shredded cheese; bake, uncovered, at 350° for about 30 minutes, or until lightly browned. Yield: 6 to 8 servings.

WHITE RICE CASSEROLE

1-1/2 cups uncooked regular rice
    1 teaspoon basil
    1 teaspoon thyme
       Salt and pepper
    1 pound pasteurized process cheese,
       shredded
    1 cup chopped parsley
    3 green onions and tops, finely chopped
  1/2 cup chopped green pepper
  1/2 cup salad oil
    2 eggs, beaten
    1 cup milk

Cook rice according to package directions, making sure it is not cooked too dry. Add basil, thyme, salt, and pepper. Stir in shredded cheese while rice is hot. Add other ingredients and mix well. Place into a greased 1-1/2-quart casserole dish and bake at 325° for 45 minutes. Yield: 6 to 8 servings.

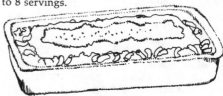

CHEESE AND NUT PUFF

    8 (1/2-inch) slices day-old white bread
    2 cups shredded sharp American cheese
  3/4 cup ground Brazil nuts
  1/2 teaspoon salt
  1/4 teaspoon dry mustard
  1/2 teaspoon paprika
    2 eggs
    2 cups milk

Remove crusts from bread; cut slices in half diagonally; place half in a 2-1/2-inch-deep, 10-inch baking dish. Sprinkle half the cheese and 1/2 cup nuts over bread; cover with a second layer of bread and cheese. Add seasonings to eggs; beat until blended. Stir in milk and pour over the bread and cheese. Sprinkle remaining nuts over top. Bake at 325° for 45 minutes. Serve at once. Yield: 6 servings.

CHEESE SOUFFLE

    1 tablespoon butter
    1 clove garlic
    5 slices white bread, buttered and cut
        into cubes
1/2 pound cheese, shredded
    4 eggs
    2 cups milk
        Hot pepper sauce to taste
    1 teaspoon Worcestershire sauce
    1 teaspoon dry mustard
        Salt and pepper

Rub a 1-quart casserole dish with butter and garlic. Then make alternate layers of cubed bread and shredded cheese. Combine eggs, milk, hot pepper sauce, Worcestershire sauce, mustard, salt, and pepper; mix well. Pour over layered bread and cheese in the prepared casserole dish. Let stand for 6 hours or more. Place casserole dish in a pan of water and bake at 300° for 1-1/2 hours. Yield: 4 to 6 servings.

CHEESE PUDDING

    8 slices white bread
1/3 cup butter or margarine
    2 cups shredded cheese
    3 cups milk
    4 eggs
1-1/3 teaspoons salt
1/3 teaspoon dry mustard

Spread the bread with butter, and cut each slice into four pieces. Alternate layers of cheese and bread in a greased, flat baking dish so that the cheese is on top. Combine milk, eggs, salt, and mustard. Pour mixture over cheese and bread. Let stand in refrigerator overnight. Bake at 325° for about 40 minutes. Yield: 8 servings.

CHEESE-RICE CASSEROLE

    3 cups cooked rice
1-1/2 cups cooked green peas
1/2 pound American cheese, shredded
    1 egg, beaten
2-1/2 cups white sauce
    2 tablespoons butter or margarine

Place rice, peas, and cheese in alternating layers in a greased casserole dish, ending with the cheese layer. Combine egg and white sauce. Pour into casserole dish. Dot with butter. Bake at 375° for about 25 minutes. Yield: 6 servings.

CHEESE CASSEROLE

    About 8 to 10 slices bread
    1 pound semisharp cheese, shredded
    4 eggs
    2 cups milk
        Salt and pepper to taste
    1 teaspoon dry mustard

Remove crusts from bread. Spread half of the cheese in the bottom of a greased 7-1/2-x 12-inch baking dish. Cover cheese with slices of bread; cut to fit so that the entire cheese layer is covered. Sprinkle remainder of cheese over bread. Beat eggs. Add milk, salt, pepper, and mustard; pour over cheese and bread mixture. Cover and refrigerate for several hours, or overnight. Bake, covered, at 325° for 45 minutes. Yield: 6 to 8 servings.

CHEESE STRATA

    3 eggs, slightly beaten
1-1/4 cups milk
1/2 teaspoon brown sugar
1/8 teaspoon paprika
    1 small onion, minced
1/4 teaspoon dry mustard
1/4 teaspoon salt
1/4 teaspoon pepper
1/4 teaspoon Worcestershire sauce
1/4 teaspoon cayenne pepper
        Softened butter or margarine
    4 slices bread
3/4 pound Cheddar cheese, shredded

Combine eggs, milk, brown sugar, paprika, onion, mustard, salt, pepper, Worcestershire sauce, and cayenne pepper. Set aside. Spread butter over slices of bread; cut off crusts and cut each slice into small squares. Arrange a layer of bread squares in a rectangular baking dish; top with cheese, and repeat layers until all bread and cheese are used. Pour egg and milk mixture over all. Cover dish and place in the refrigerator for 4 hours, or overnight. Take out of refrigerator 30 minutes before baking. Bake at 300° for 1 hour. Yield: 6 to 8 servings.

BAKED DEVILED EGG CASSEROLE

    6 hard-cooked eggs
    2 teaspoons prepared mustard
    3 tablespoons commercial sour cream
  1/4 teaspoon salt
    2 tablespoons butter or margarine
  1/2 cup chopped green pepper
  1/3 cup chopped onion
  1/4 cup chopped pimiento
    1 (10-3/4-ounce) can cream of
       mushroom soup
  3/4 cup commercial sour cream
  1/2 cup shredded Cheddar cheese

Cut eggs in half lengthwise; remove yolks. Mash together the yolks, mustard, 3 tablespoons sour cream, and salt. Fill egg whites with yolk mixture.

Melt butter in a large skillet; sauté green pepper and onion until tender. Remove from heat; stir in pimiento, soup, and 3/4 cup sour cream. Place half the soup mixture in a greased 1-1/2-quart shallow baking dish; arrange eggs, cut side up, in a single layer in the dish. Pour remaining soup mixture over top; sprinkle with cheese. Bake at 350° for 20 minutes, or until heated through. Casserole may be prepared in advance; refrigerate until ready to bake. Yield: 12 servings.

EGGS 'N CHIPS CASSEROLE

    8 hard-cooked eggs, coarsely chopped
  1-1/2 cups diced celery
  1/4 cup coarsely chopped walnuts
    2 tablespoons minced green pepper
    1 teaspoon minced onion
  1/2 teaspoon salt
  1/4 teaspoon pepper
  2/3 cup mayonnaise or salad dressing
    1 cup shredded Cheddar cheese
    1 cup crushed potato chips

Combine eggs, celery, walnuts, green pepper, onion, salt, pepper, and mayonnaise. Toss lightly, but mix thoroughly. Place in a greased 1-1/2-quart baking dish. Sprinkle with shredded cheese and top with potato chips. Bake at 375° for 25 minutes, or until thoroughly heated. Yield: 6 servings.

SAVORY EGGS

    1 cup shredded American cheese
    2 tablespoons butter or margarine
  1/2 cup cream
  1/4 teaspoon salt
  1/4 teaspoon pepper
    1 teaspoon prepared mustard
    6 eggs, slightly beaten

Spread cheese in the bottom of a greased shallow 8-inch round or square baking dish. Dot with butter. Combine cream, salt, pepper, and mustard. Pour half this mixture over cheese. Pour eggs into baking dish. Add remaining cream mixture. Bake at 325° for about 25 minutes. Yield: 6 servings.

SWISS EGGS

    1 tablespoon butter or margarine
    4 very thin slices cheese
    4 eggs
       Salt and pepper to taste
    3 tablespoons cream
    2 tablespoons shredded cheese

Melt butter in a shallow baking dish. Cut the slices of cheese in pieces to cover the bottom of the baking dish. Break eggs and drop them into the dish over the cheese. Season to taste and pour cream over eggs. Sprinkle cheese on top and bake at 300° until eggs are set and cheese is a delicate brown, about 15 to 20 minutes. Yield: 2 to 3 servings.

BAKED MACARONI AND CHEESE

    1 (8-ounce) package elbow macaroni
    3 tablespoons butter or margarine
    2 tablespoons all-purpose flour
    1 teaspoon salt
  1/8 teaspoon pepper
    2 cups milk
    2 cups shredded sharp Cheddar cheese
    1 tablespoon grated onion
    1 teaspoon dry mustard
    1 teaspoon Worcestershire sauce
  1/2 cup buttered breadcrumbs

Cook macaroni according to package directions; drain and set aside. Melt butter; blend in flour, salt, and pepper. Add milk and cook over low heat until smooth and thickened, stirring constantly. Add cheese, onion, dry mustard, and Worcestershire sauce; continue to cook until cheese melts. Add cooked macaroni. Place in a greased 2-quart casserole dish. Top with crumbs. Bake at 375° for 25 minutes, or until browned. Yield: 6 to 8 servings.

MACARONI AND BROCCOLI CASSEROLE

      3 tablespoons butter or margarine
      3 tablespoons all-purpose flour
  1-1/2 teaspoons salt
    1/8 teaspoon pepper
  1-1/2 cups milk
    1/4 to 1/2 cup shredded cheese
    3/4 cup mayonnaise
      1 (8-ounce) package macaroni
      2 cups chopped, cooked broccoli

Melt butter; stir in flour, salt, and pepper.
Add milk gradually, stirring constantly. Cook
until thickened, stirring often. Remove from
heat and stir in cheese and mayonnaise. Cook
macaroni in boiling, salted water according to
package directions. Cook just until tender; do
not overcook. Drain, rinse, and drain again.
Place a layer of macaroni, then a layer of
chopped, cooked broccoli in a greased 1-1/2-
quart casserole dish. Pour sauce over broccoli.
Repeat layers, ending with sauce. Bake at 350°
for about 20 minutes, or until thoroughly heated.
Yield: 6 to 8 servings.

MACARONI AND CHEESE

    1/3 cup elbow macaroni
      2 cups boiling salted water
      1 egg
    1/3 cup evaporated milk
    1/2 cup shredded Cheddar cheese
        Seasonings as desired
        Shredded Cheddar cheese
        Paprika

Add 1/3 cup macaroni to boiling salted water
and cook for about 15 minutes; rinse and drain.
Beat egg and milk together; add to cooked
macaroni along with 1/2 cup cheese. Add
seasonings as desired, and turn mixture into a
greased 1/2-quart baking dish. Sprinkle with
additional cheese and paprika. Bake at 350° for
25 to 30 minutes. Yield: 2 servings.

QUICK MACARONI AND CHEESE

      2 tablespoons butter or margarine
      2 tablespoons all-purpose flour
  1-1/2 cups milk
      2 eggs
      1 cup shredded Cheddar cheese
    1/2 teaspoon Worcestershire sauce
      3 drops hot pepper sauce
  1-1/2 cups cooked macaroni

Melt butter in the top of a double boiler; add
flour, and stir until well blended. Reserve 2
tablespoons of the milk to mix with eggs. Pour
remaining milk gradually into butter and flour
mixture, stirring constantly. Cook until smooth.
Pour gradually into slightly beaten eggs mixed
with milk. Add cheese, and stir until melted.
Add Worcestershire sauce and hot pepper sauce;
pour over macaroni in a greased 1-1/2-quart
baking dish. Bake at 350° for 35 minutes.
Yield: 6 servings.

CHEESE-NOODLE CASSEROLE

      3 cups uncooked noodles
    1/4 cup butter or margarine
      3 tablespoons all-purpose flour
    3/4 teaspoon salt
    1/4 teaspoon garlic salt
    1/8 teaspoon white pepper
        Dash ground nutmeg
      2 cups milk
    1/2 cup dry white wine
      1 (8-ounce) package pasteurized process
        Swiss cheese, shredded
      2 tablespoons sliced green onion
      2 tablespoons diced pimiento
    1/2 cup grated Parmesan cheese

Cook noodles according to package directions;
drain and set aside. Melt butter; blend in flour,
salt, garlic salt, pepper, and nutmeg. Add milk
and cook, stirring constantly, until sauce is
smooth and thickened. Add wine and Swiss
cheese; stir until cheese is melted. Fold in cooked
noodles, green onion, pimiento, and 1/4 cup
Parmesan cheese. Pour mixture into a greased,
shallow 1-1/2-quart casserole dish. Sprinkle
with remaining Parmesan cheese. Bake at 350°
for 25 minutes, or until hot and bubbly around
the edges. Yield: 6 servings.

NOODLE-RICE CASSEROLE

      1 (4-ounce) package extremely fine noodles
    1/2 cup butter or margarine
      1 cup regular uncooked long-grain rice
        About 1 cup chicken broth
      1 (10-1/2-ounce) can onion soup
      2 tablespoons soy sauce
        Sliced toasted almonds

Sauté raw noodles in butter in a saucepan
until just golden. Add all other ingredients
except almonds. Cover and simmer until rice is
done, about 30 minutes, adding a little more
broth if necessary to keep rice moist. Turn into
a buttered casserole dish; sprinkle with almonds
and bake, uncovered, at 325° for 30 minutes.
Yield: 6 to 8 servings.

VEGETABLE CASSEROLES

ASPARAGUS-ALMOND CASSEROLE

    1 (14-1/2-ounce) can green asparagus
1/2 to 1 cup crushed potato chips
1/3 cup chopped almonds
    1 (10-3/4-ounce) can cream of
        mushroom soup
        Milk (optional)

Place a layer of asparagus in a greased 1-quart casserole dish, then add a layer of potato chips, then chopped almonds. Repeat. Pour mushroom soup over all. If soup is very thick, add small amount of milk. Bake at 375° for 15 minutes. Yield: 4 to 6 servings.

ASPARAGUS DELUXE

    1 (14-1/2-ounce) can green asparagus,
        drained and liquid reserved
    3 tablespoons butter or margarine
    3 tablespoons cornstarch
3/4 cup asparagus juice
3/4 cup milk
    2 hard-cooked eggs, sliced
    1 cup shredded Cheddar cheese
1/2 cup buttered breadcrumbs

Drain asparagus and set aside. Melt butter, add cornstarch, and heat to the bubbly stage. Add asparagus juice and milk; cook over low heat, stirring constantly. Layer asparagus, egg slices, cheese, and sauce in a greased 1-quart casserole dish. Repeat layers and top with breadcrumbs. Bake at 325° for 30 minutes. Yield: 6 servings.

ASPARAGUS CASSEROLE

    2 tablespoons butter or margarine
    2 tablespoons all-purpose flour
    2 (14-1/2-ounce) cans green asparagus
        tips, drained and liquid reserved
    1 cup light cream
        Salt and pepper to taste
        Dash paprika
1/2 cup shredded Cheddar cheese
    1 (4-ounce) can mushroom pieces
1/2 to 3/4 cup cracker crumbs
        Hard-cooked eggs, sliced

Melt butter in a small skillet. Stir in flour; when well blended, stir in 2 tablespoons asparagus liquid to make a paste. Stir in cream; cook and stir constantly until mixture thickens. Add salt and pepper to taste. Stir in paprika, shredded cheese, and mushroom pieces; continue stirring until cheese is melted.

Line the bottom of a greased 2-quart casserole dish with half of the asparagus tips. Cover with half of the sauce. Add another layer of asparagus and top with the rest of the sauce. Spread cracker crumbs over casserole. Let cool; cover tightly and freeze. Casserole may be stored in the freezer for 3 months.

Remove casserole from the freezer; thaw; cover top with sliced hard-cooked eggs and bake at 350° for about 15 minutes. Yield: 6 to 8 servings.

ASPARAGUS-WATER CHESTNUT CASSEROLE

    2 (14-1/2-ounce) cans cut asparagus,
        drained
    1 (8-ounce) can water chestnuts, finely
        sliced
    1 (10-3/4-ounce) can cream of
        mushroom soup
        Buttered breadcrumbs

Place alternate layers of asparagus and water chestnuts in a greased glass baking dish. Pour soup over layers. Top with buttered breadcrumbs. Bake at 350° for 30 minutes. Yield: 4 to 6 servings.

ASPARAGUS-EGG CASSEROLE

    2 tablespoons butter or margarine
    2 tablespoons all-purpose flour
1/2 teaspoon salt
    Dash pepper
    1 cup milk
    1 cup shredded American cheese
    1 cup buttered breadcrumbs
    4 hard-cooked eggs, sliced
    2 cups cooked, fresh or canned, asparagus

Make white sauce of butter, flour, salt, pepper, and milk. Stir in cheese. Place half of the buttered breadcrumbs in a greased 1-1/2-quart casserole dish. Place alternate layers of eggs, cooked asparagus, and cheese sauce over the breadcrumbs. Cover top with the remaining breadcrumbs. Bake at 350° for 15 minutes. Yield: 8 servings.

ASPARAGUS MILANO

    1 (14-1/2-ounce) can green asparagus, drained
1/2 cup butter or margarine, melted
    1 (1-3/8-ounce) envelope onion soup mix
    1 cup diced Mozzarella cheese
    2 tablespoons grated Parmesan cheese

Pour asparagus into a greased baking dish. Combine butter and onion soup mix; pour over asparagus. Top with cheese. Bake at 350° for 10 minutes, or until cheese melts and browns lightly. Yield: 4 servings.

ASPARAGUS, PEAS, AND MUSHROOM CASSEROLE

    2 (10-ounce) packages frozen asparagus spears
    2 (10-ounce) packages frozen peas
    1 (10-3/4-ounce) can cream of mushroom soup
3/4 cup shredded sharp Cheddar cheese
    2 tablespoons melted butter or margarine
    1 cup soft breadcrumbs

Cook asparagus and peas according to the package directions; drain. Arrange half of the asparagus in a greased 2-quart casserole dish. In a bowl, gently mix peas, soup, and cheese. Spoon half the mixture over the asparagus layer. Add remaining asparagus; top with remaining pea mixture. Stir melted butter into crumbs; sprinkle over top of the casserole. Bake at 350° for 30 minutes. Yield: 8 servings.

BAKED BEANS WITH CHEESE SWIRLS

    2 (1-pound) cans baked beans
    1 small onion, minced
1/3 cup finely chopped celery
1/3 cup milk
    1 cup commercial biscuit mix
2/3 cup shredded sharp Cheddar cheese
    2 tablespoons diced pimiento

Empty 1 can of baked beans into a shallow casserole dish. Sprinkle with minced onion and celery; add second can of beans. Bake at 400° while preparing cheese swirls.

Add milk to biscuit mix; mix and knead lightly. Roll out into an oblong about 6 x 8 inches. Sprinkle with cheese and pimiento; roll up like a jelly roll, sealing edge. Cut into 6 or 8 slices and arrange over beans. Continue baking for 25 minutes, or until swirls are done. Yield: 6 to 8 servings.

HAWAIIAN-STYLE BAKED BEANS

    2 (1-pound) cans pork and beans
1/4 pound cooked ham, diced
1/2 teaspoon dry mustard
1/4 cup brown sugar, firmly packed
    2 tablespoons finely chopped onion
    1 cup pineapple chunks, drained and liquid reserved
1/4 cup pineapple juice

Grease a 1-1/2-quart baking dish. Spoon 1 can of pork and beans into the bottom of the dish. Combine ham, mustard, brown sugar, onion, pineapple, pineapple juice; spoon over layer of beans, and top with the remaining can of pork and beans. Cover and bake at 350° for 1 hour. Yield: 5 to 6 servings.

ONION-BEAN BAKE

    4 frankfurters, sliced
    2 (1-pound) cans pork and beans
    1 cup shredded Cheddar cheese
    2 tablespoons brown sugar
    2 teaspoons parsley flakes
1/2 teaspoon seasoned salt
    1 (3-ounce) can French fried onion rings

Combine frankfurters, beans, cheese, brown sugar, parsley flakes, and seasoned salt. Stir in 1/2 can onion rings. Spoon mixture into a greased 1-1/2-quart casserole dish. Bake at 350° for about 25 minutes. Sprinkle top with remaining onion rings, and bake for 5 minutes longer. Yield: 8 servings.

EASY GREEN BEAN CASSEROLE

- 1 (10-3/4-ounce) can cream of mushroom soup
  Dash pepper
- 1 teaspoon soy sauce (optional)
- 2 (16-ounce) cans green beans, drained
- 2 (3-ounce) cans French fried onions
- 1/2 cup shredded Cheddar cheese

Combine soup, pepper, and soy sauce. Place beans in a greased casserole dish in layers with soup mixture and 1 can onions. Cover and bake at 350° for 20 minutes. Sprinkle with remaining onions and cheese. Bake 5 minutes longer. Yield: 6 to 8 servings.

GREEN BEAN CASSEROLE

- 1 medium onion, diced
- 2 tablespoons butter or margarine
- 2 tablespoons all-purpose flour
- 2 tablespoons water
- 1 teaspoon salt
- 1/2 teaspoon pepper
- 2 tablespoons freshly squeezed lemon juice
- 2 (16-ounce) cans green beans, drained
- 1 cup commercial sour cream
- 1/2 cup shredded Cheddar cheese
- 1/2 cup dry breadcrumbs

Sauté onion in butter. Gradually stir in flour, water, salt, pepper, and lemon juice; simmer for 3 minutes. Add beans and sour cream; place in a 2-quart casserole dish. Sprinkle with cheese and crumbs. Bake at 350° for 30 minutes. Yield: 8 servings.

LIMA BEAN CASSEROLE

- 1/2 pound dried lima beans
  Water
- 4 slices bacon, diced
- 2 medium onions, sliced
- 2/3 teaspoon salt
- 1/4 teaspoon pepper
- 1/2 teaspoon poultry seasoning
- 1 cup milk
- 1 cup buttered breadcrumbs

Soak beans overnight in water to cover. In the morning, bring water slowly to boiling point. Simmer until beans are tender but not broken; drain. Cook bacon; remove from pan; cook onions in bacon drippings. Grease a deep baking dish; arrange layers of beans, seasonings, and diced bacon. Repeat until all ingredients are used. Pour in milk, sprinkle buttered breadcrumbs over all, and bake at 375° for 25 to 30 minutes. Yield: 4 servings.

CURRIED LIMA BEANS IN CASSEROLE

- 2 (10-ounce) packages frozen baby lima beans
- 2 slices bacon, diced
- 1 medium onion, minced
- 1 clove garlic, crushed
- 1/2 teaspoon curry powder
- 1 (10-3/4-ounce) can cream of mushroom soup
- 1/2 cup commercial sour cream
- 2 tablespoons dry white wine, sherry or milk
- 1 (3-1/2-ounce) can French fried onions

Cook beans according to package directions until just tender. Drain. Fry bacon until crisp in a skillet; drain on paper towels. Sauté onion, garlic, and curry powder for about 5 minutes in the bacon drippings remaining in the skillet. Blend soup, sour cream, and wine in a bowl until smooth. Add to skillet; heat to just under boiling point; stir in beans and bacon bits. Turn into a greased 1-1/2-quart shallow casserole dish, and top with slightly crushed French fried onions. Bake at 325° for about 25 minutes. Yield: 6 to 8 servings.

DIXIE CASSEROLE

- 1-1/2 cups dried lima beans
- 4 cups water
- 4 teaspoons salt, divided
- 6 pork chops
- 2 tablespoons all-purpose flour
- 1/3 cup catsup
- 2 tablespoons brown sugar
- 2 tablespoons dehydrated onion flakes
- 1/2 teaspoon dry mustard
- 1/4 teaspoon pepper
- 1/8 teaspoon garlic powder
- 1 bay leaf

Soak lima beans overnight in water. Add 3 teaspoons salt. Bring to boiling point and simmer for 1 hour, or until beans are almost soft. Drain off water and save. Place beans in a greased 2-1/2-quart casserole dish. Rub remaining salt on both sides of pork chops. Sprinkle chops with flour and brown on both sides. Place over beans. Mix 1-1/2 cups of the bean water, catsup, sugar, onion flakes, mustard, pepper, garlic powder, and bay leaf. Pour over beans and pork chops. Cover and bake at 325° for 1 hour, or until done. Remove cover and bake an additional 30 minutes. Yield: 6 servings.

LIMA BEANS AND MUSHROOM CASEROLE

- 1 onion, coarsely chopped
- 6 tablespoons butter or margarine, divided
- 2 (10-ounce) packages frozen lima beans
- 1 tablespoon sugar
- 1/2 teaspoon salt
- 1/4 teaspoon pepper
- 1 (8-ounce) can sliced mushrooms
- 1 tablespoon water
- 3 tablespoons all-purpose flour
- 3 cups light cream or milk
- 1/4 cup dry sherry
- 2 egg yolks, lightly beaten
- 1/2 teaspoon salt
- 1/2 teaspoon pepper
- 1/4 cup shredded mild American cheese

Sauté onion in 2 tablespoons butter until transparent; add beans. Cover and cook for 5 minutes. Use a fork to separate beans. Add sugar, salt, pepper, mushrooms, and water. Cover again and cook until beans are tender.

Melt remaining butter in a separate pan. Add flour and cook until bubbly. Add cream and cook, stirring frequently, until sauce begins to thicken. Remove from heat; add sherry, egg yolks, salt, and pepper. Combine with lima beans and mushroom mixture. Pour into a greased 1-1/2-quart casserole dish and sprinkle with cheese. Cool, wrap, and freeze. To serve, bake for 1 hour at 350°. To serve without freezing, cut baking time to 35 to 45 minutes. Yield: 6 to 8 servings.

BROCCOLI CASSEROLE

- 2 (10-ounce) packages frozen broccoli
- 2 tablespoons butter or margarine, melted
- 2 tablespoons all-purpose flour
- 1 teaspoon salt
- 2 cups milk
- 1/4 teaspoon pepper
- 3/4 cup shredded cheese
- 1/4 cup chopped almonds
- 1/2 cup buttered breadcrumbs
- 4 slices bacon

Cook broccoli according to package directions until just tender. Drain and place in a greased casserole dish. Make a sauce of the butter, flour, salt, milk, pepper, and cheese. Sprinkle almonds over the broccoli; pour sauce over all. Sprinkle top with breadcrumbs and bacon. Bake at 350° for 20 minutes, or until bubbling hot and browned on top. Yield: 8 servings.

BROCCOLI-PEAS CASSEROLE

- 2 (10-ounce) packages frozen chopped broccoli
- 1 (17-ounce) can green peas
- 1 (10-3/4-ounce) can cream of mushroom soup
- 1 cup mayonnaise
- 1 teaspoon salt
- 1/2 teaspoon pepper
- 1 cup shredded sharp Cheddar cheese
- 1 medium onion, chopped
- 2 eggs, beaten
- 1/2 cup crushed round crackers

Cook broccoli according to package directions. Drain. Arrange 1 package of cooked broccoli in a greased 2-quart casserole dish. Cover with peas. Mix mushroom soup, mayonnaise, salt, pepper, cheese, onion, and eggs to make sauce. Pour half of the sauce over the broccoli and peas. Add remaining broccoli and top with remaining sauce. Sprinkle crushed crackers on top. Bake at 350° for 30 minutes. Yield: 8 servings.

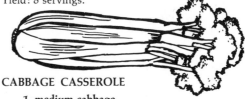

CABBAGE CASSEROLE

- 1 medium cabbage
  Boiling salted water
- 4 tablespoons butter or margarine, melted
- 4 tablespoons all-purpose flour
- 1/2 teaspoon salt
- 1/4 teaspoon pepper
- 2 cups milk
- 1/2 green pepper, chopped
- 1/2 medium onion, chopped
- 2/3 cup shredded Cheddar cheese
- 1/2 cup mayonnaise
- 3 tablespoons chili sauce

Cut cabbage into wedges; boil in salted water until tender, about 15 minutes. Drain cabbage and place in a greased 13- x 9- x 2-inch casserole dish. Combine butter and flour in a saucepan over low heat; stir until smooth and bubbly. Add salt, pepper, and milk. Stir constantly over medium heat until sauce is smooth and thick. Pour sauce over cabbage in the casserole dish and bake at 375° for 20 minutes. Combine green pepper, onion, cheese, mayonnaise, and chili sauce; mix well and spread over cabbage. Bake at 400° for 20 minutes. Yield: 8 to 10 servings.

SCALLOPED CABBAGE AND APPLES

2 quarts shredded cabbage
1 quart tart sliced apples
2 teaspoons salt
2 to 4 tablespoons melted butter or
 margarine
4 tablespoons sugar
1 cup buttered breadcrumbs

In a greased 2-quart baking dish, place alternate layers of the cabbage and apples, seasoning each layer with salt and butter, and sprinkle sugar on the apples. Spread buttered breadcrumbs over the last layer. Cover and bake at 350° for 45 minutes, or until cabbage and apples are tender. Remove the cover during the last 10 minutes to brown the crumbs. Serve from the baking dish. Yield: 6 servings.

CARROT-BRUSSELS SPROUTS CASSEROLE

4 large carrots, sliced
2 (10-ounce) packages frozen Brussels
 sprouts
1/2 cup boiling water
1 teaspoon salt
1 (10-3/4-ounce) can cream of
 mushroom soup
1/2 cup shredded cheese

Simmer carrots and Brussels sprouts in boiling salted water until tender. Add soup and cheese; stir lightly. Place in a greased casserole dish and bake at 350° until bubbly. Yield: 6 to 8 servings.

CARROT CASSEROLE

1 (10-3/4-ounce) can cream of
 mushroom soup
1/2 onion, finely chopped
2 (16-ounce) cans diced or shoestring
 carrots
1/2 cup crushed potato chips

Combine mushroom soup and onion. Alternate layers of carrots with soup and onion mixture in a greased 1-quart casserole dish. Bake at 325° for 20 to 25 minutes, or until thoroughly heated. Just before removing from oven, sprinkle with crushed potato chips and brown slightly. Yield: 4 servings.

Tarragon

Tarragon, a versatile herb, is an important seasoning in seafood, poultry, and veal casseroles. Add a pinch to egg and cheese dishes.

CARROT SURPRISES

1-1/3 cups chopped onion
1/4 cup butter or margarine
2 cups soft breadcrumbs
1/2 teaspoon salt
1/3 cup shredded American cheese
2 tablespoons water
2-1/2 cups cooked sliced carrots
 Butter or margarine

Brown onion in 1/4 cup butter; mix with breadcrumbs, salt, cheese, and water. Place 1 cup carrots in a greased 1-quart casserole dish; cover with the breadcrumb mixture. Arrange the remaining carrots in overlapping circles around the edge of the casserole. Dot with butter and bake at 350° for 20 minutes. Yield: 6 servings.

CREAMED CAULIFLOWER AND PEAS

3 (10-ounce) packages frozen cauliflower
1 (10-ounce) package frozen peas
1/4 cup water
1/4 teaspoon salt
 Milk
3/4 cup finely chopped onion
1/4 cup butter or margarine
3 tablespoons all-purpose flour
1/2 teaspoon salt
1/4 teaspoon pepper
1/4 teaspoon ground nutmeg
1 cup half-and-half
1/4 cup buttered breadcrumbs

Cook cauliflower according to package directions; drain. Put peas, water, and 1/4 teaspoon salt in a saucepan; bring to boil, reduce heat, cover, and simmer for 5 minutes. Drain peas, reserving liquid. Add enough milk to liquid to make 1 cup. Set aside.

Sauté onion in butter until golden. Remove from heat; stir in flour, 1/2 teaspoon salt, pepper, and nutmeg. Gradually stir in reserved liquid and half-and-half; bring to a boil, stirring constantly.

Combine cauliflower, peas, and sauce in a greased 2-quart casserole dish. Top with breadcrumbs. Cover and refrigerate overnight. Cover and bake at 400° for 30 minutes; uncover and bake an additional 20 minutes, or until bubbly. Yield: 8 to 10 servings.

Cumin

Cumin adds a pungent tang to meat dishes, beans, and sauces.

CELERY AND POTATO CASSEROLE

3 cups thinly sliced celery
3 cups thinly sliced raw potatoes
1-1/2 cups thinly sliced onions
3 tablespoons all-purpose flour
1/2 cup milk
1/4 cup butter or margarine
1-3/4 teaspoons salt
1/8 teaspoon pepper

Alternate layers of celery, potatoes, and onions in a greased 6-cup casserole dish. Sprinkle flour evenly over each layer. Combine remaining ingredients; heat and pour over the casserole. Cover and bake at 350° for 30 minutes. Remove cover and continue baking until top is brown, about 15 to 20 minutes. Yield: 6 servings.

CORN AND GREEN BEAN CASSEROLE

1 (4-1/2-ounce) can deviled ham
3/4 teaspoon paprika
2 teaspoons all-purpose flour
1-3/4 cups half-and-half
1 teaspoon grated onion
3/4 teaspoon salt
1/4 teaspoon pepper
2 (16-ounce) cans green beans
1 (17-ounce) can whole kernel corn
1/2 cup commercial sour cream

Heat deviled ham in a skillet. Add paprika, flour, half-and-half, onion, and seasonings. Heat and stir until thickened. Heat and drain green beans and corn. Add to sauce, along with sour cream. Serve immediately. Yield: 6 servings.

CORN SOUFFLE

4 tablespoons butter or margarine
4 tablespoons all-purpose flour
1-1/2 cups milk
1 teaspoon salt
1/8 teaspoon cayenne pepper
1 cup whole kernel corn
2 tablespoons chopped pimiento
1-1/2 teaspoons Worcestershire sauce
1/2 teaspoon prepared mustard
1 teaspoon onion juice
6 eggs, separated

Melt butter in a saucepan. Add flour and blend. Gradually add milk, salt, and cayenne pepper. Cook over low heat, stirring occasionally, until thickened and smooth. Remove from heat; add remaining ingredients except eggs. Mix lightly. Add beaten egg yolks, blend, and allow to cool. Fold in stiffly beaten egg whites and pour into a 2-quart casserole dish. Cut around the mixture with a knife (about 2 inches from the edge), and bake at 350° for 1-1/2 hours. Serve at once. Yield: 6 servings.

CRUNCHY-TOPPED SCALLOPED CORN

1/4 cup finely chopped onion
1/4 cup finely chopped green pepper
2 tablespoons butter or margarine
2 tablespoons all-purpose flour
1 teaspoon salt
1/2 teaspoon paprika
1/4 teaspoon dry mustard
Dash pepper
3/4 cup milk
1 (1-pound) can whole kernel corn, drained
1 egg, slightly beaten
1 cup corn flakes
1 tablespoon butter or margarine, melted

Sauté onion and green pepper in 2 tablespoons butter until golden brown. Blend in flour and seasonings; cook until bubbly. Remove from heat; stir in milk gradually. Return to heat and bring to a boil; boil for 1 minute, stirring constantly. Remove from heat; add corn and egg. Pour into a greased 1-quart baking dish. Coat corn flakes with 1 tablespoon melted butter; sprinkle over corn mixture. Bake at 350° for 20 to 30 minutes. Yield: 6 to 8 servings.

ELEGANT SCALLOPED CORN

1 (17-ounce) can cream-style corn
1 cup cracker crumbs
1/2 cup diced celery
1/4 cup diced onion
3/4 cup cubed American cheese
1 teaspoon salt
2 eggs, well-beaten
2 tablespoons melted butter or margarine
1 cup milk
Parsley
1/4 teaspoon paprika

Combine corn, cracker crumbs, celery, onion, cheese, salt, eggs, butter, and milk. Pour into a greased 2-quart casserole dish, and bake at 350° for 50 minutes. Garnish with parsley; sprinkle paprika on top. Yield: 8 servings.

SOUTHWESTERN CORN SCALLOP

2 eggs, slightly beaten
1 (17-ounce) can cream-style corn
3/4 cup milk
1/2 cup coarsely crushed crackers
1 cup shredded sharp Cheddar cheese
1 tablespoon chopped canned green chili peppers
1 teaspoon sugar
1 teaspoon salt
1/8 teaspoon pepper

Combine all ingredients and place in a greased 1-quart casserole dish. Bake at 350° for 60 minutes. Yield: 8 servings.

GREEN CHILE-HOMINY CASSEROLE

2 (16-ounce) cans hominy, drained
3 tablespoons butter or margarine, melted
3 tablespoons all-purpose flour
1 (8-ounce) can green chiles (use less if desired)
    Milk
1 tablespoon chopped pimiento
1-1/2 cups shredded sharp Cheddar cheese

Place hominy in an oblong, buttered casserole dish; set aside. Combine butter and flour in a saucepan; heat and stir until smooth. Drain juice from chiles and add enough milk to make 2 cups; add liquid to flour mixture. Continue to stir over low heat until well blended. Add chiles and pimiento. Pour sauce over hominy; sprinkle with cheese. Bake at 350° for 30 minutes. (Chiles make this casserole very hot.) Yield: 8 servings.

HOMINY CASSEROLE

4 slices bacon
    Shortening
6 tablespoons all-purpose flour
1 teaspoon sugar
1 teaspoon salt
1 teaspoon chili powder
2-1/4 cups tomatoes
3 cups cooked hominy
2 cups onion rings
1 cup shredded American cheese

Sauté bacon in a large frying pan until crisp; set aside. Add enough shortening to bacon drippings in pan to make 4 tablespoons. Blend in flour, sugar, salt, and chili powder; stir in tomatoes and cook, stirring constantly, until mixture is thick. Layer hominy, onion rings, and tomato mixture in a greased 2-quart baking dish. Sprinkle with cheese and top with bacon slices. Bake at 325° for about 25 minutes. Yield: 6 servings.

CHEESY EGGPLANT CASSEROLE

2 large eggplants, peeled and sliced
3/4 cup soft breadcrumbs
2 teaspoons grated onion
2 tablespoons catsup
1 teaspoon salt
1/8 teaspoon pepper
    Dash Worcestershire sauce
2 beaten eggs
2 tablespoons butter or margarine
2 tablespoons all-purpose flour
3/4 cup milk
1 cup cubed Cheddar cheese

Boil peeled and sliced eggplant in water until well cooked. Drain, mash, and mix with breadcrumbs, onion, catsup, salt, pepper, Worcestershire sauce, and eggs. Melt butter, stir in flour, and add milk. Cook until mixture thickens. Add to eggplant mixture. Place in a buttered casserole dish, sprinkle with cheese, and bake at 350° for 30 to 40 minutes. Eggplant should be browned slightly and cheese well melted before removing from the oven. Yield: 6 servings.

Note: To freeze, mix all ingredients except cheese and freeze in plastic freezer containers. Add cheese when ready to bake.

EGGPLANT CASSEROLE DELIGHT

1 (1-1/2-pound) eggplant
3 medium onions, chopped
1 cup water
2 tablespoons butter or margarine, melted
2 egg yolks, beaten
1 teaspoon salt
1/2 cup dry breadcrumbs
1/2 cup water
1/2 cup grated Parmesan cheese

Pare eggplant and cut into small pieces. Boil eggplant and onions in 1 cup water until tender, stirring occasionally. Drain and mash; stir in butter, egg yolks, salt, breadcrumbs, and water. Spoon mixture into a greased 1-1/2-quart casserole dish. Bake at 350° for 20 minutes. Sprinkle grated Parmesan cheese on top and bake for an additional 10 minutes. Yield: 6 servings.

Chervil

Chervil looks and tastes like mild parsley. Sweet and aromatic, it combines excellently with other herbs. Chervil gives a delicious flavor to roasts, soups, salads, sauces, egg and chicken dishes, and vegetables.

EGGPLANT PATRICE

- 1 small eggplant
- 4 medium tomatoes, sliced
- 2 medium green peppers, chopped
- 2 medium onions, chopped
- 1/2 teaspoon salt
- 1/4 teaspoon pepper
- 1/4 teaspoon garlic salt
  Dash monosodium glutamate (optional)
- 3/4 pound sharp Cheddar cheese, sliced
  1/8 inch thick

Slice unpeeled eggplant about 1/4 inch thick. Parboil until partially tender. Place a layer of eggplant slices in a greased 13- x 9- x 2-inch baking dish. Add a layer of sliced tomatoes. Fill spaces with a mixture of peppers and onions. Sprinkle with salt, pepper, garlic salt, and monosodium glutamate. Add a layer of cheese. Repeat layers until casserole is filled, ending with cheese. Cover and bake at 400° until mixture is steaming. Remove cover; reduce heat to 350° and bake for about 30 to 45 minutes, or until eggplant is tender and sauce is thick and golden brown. Yield: 6 servings.

EGGPLANT SUPREME

- 1 medium or large eggplant
  Salt and pepper
- 1 small onion, diced
- 2 tablespoons butter
- 3/4 cup milk
- 3 tablespoons shredded sharp cheese
- 1 cup crushed crackers
- 4 slices American cheese (optional)

Pare and slice eggplant; cook in salted water until tender. Drain and mash. Add other ingredients except cheese slices. Place in a greased 1-quart casserole dish. Bake at 350° for 40 minutes. Arrange cheese slices on top and bake for an additional 20 minutes. Yield: 4 servings.

ITALIAN EGGPLANT

- 2 cups cooked noodles
- 2 cups chopped fresh tomatoes
- 1 cup thinly sliced green pepper
- 1/4 cup all-purpose flour
  Salt and pepper to taste
- 1 medium eggplant, sliced and chopped
- 1/2 cup beef broth or bouillon
- 1/2 cup shredded sharp Cheddar cheese
- 2 tablespoons butter or margarine
- 1/2 cup cracker crumbs

Grease a 2-quart casserole dish. Place noodles, tomatoes, and green pepper in layers; sprinkle flour, salt, and pepper on each layer. Cover with chopped, sliced eggplant. Pour beef broth over mixture, and sprinkle top with shredded cheese. Dot with butter and top with cracker crumbs. Bake at 300° for about 1 hour. Yield: 6 servings.

BAKED RATATOUILLE CASSEROLE

- 2 large onions, sliced
- 2 large cloves garlic, minced
- 1 medium eggplant, cut into 1/4-inch cubes
- 6 medium zucchini, thickly sliced
- 2 green peppers, seeded and cut into chunks
- 4 large tomatoes, cut into chunks
- 2 teaspoons salt
- 1 teaspoon basil
- 1/2 cup minced parsley
- 4 tablespoons olive oil

Layer onions, garlic, eggplant, zucchini, peppers, and tomatoes in a greased 5- to 6-quart casserole dish. Sprinkle a little salt, basil, and parsley between each layer. Drizzle olive oil over the top layer. Cover and bake at 350° for 3 hours. Baste the top occasionally with some of the liquid. If it becomes soupy, uncover during the last hour of cooking to let the juices cook down.

Mix gently after removing from the oven. Add salt to taste. This may be served hot, cold, or reheated, and it is good to serve as a buffet dish for a crowd. Yield: 12 to 15 generous servings.

FIESTA CASSEROLE

- 2 (17-ounce) cans cream-style corn
- 2 (17-ounce) cans whole kernel corn
- 1/4 cup chopped olives
- 1/4 cup chopped pimiento
- 1/4 cup chopped onion
- 1/4 cup chopped green pepper
- 2 eggs, beaten
  Dash pepper
- 1 teaspoon salt
  Dash hot pepper sauce
- 1 cup cracker crumbs

Combine corn, olives, pimiento, onion, and green pepper with eggs and seasonings. Add cracker crumbs, mix thoroughly, and pour into a greased 2-quart baking dish. Bake at 350° for 30 minutes. Yield: 8 servings.

BAKED VEGETABLE CASSEROLE

1-1/2 cups milk, scalded
    1 cup dry breadcrumbs
  1/4 cup melted butter or margarine
  1/2 teaspoon salt
    1 tablespoon chopped parsley
    2 pimientos, chopped
      Dash paprika
1-1/2 tablespoons chopped onion
    3 eggs, beaten
    1 to 2 cups frozen, mixed vegetables
1-1/2 cups shredded cheese

Pour scalded milk over breadcrumbs; stir to moisten. Add butter, salt, parsley, pimiento, paprika, onion, and eggs. Mix well. Place thawed vegetables in a greased 1-quart baking dish. Pour sauce over vegetables. Sprinkle cheese on top. Place dish in a pan of water and bake at 325° for 1 to 1-1/4 hours. Yield: 4 to 6 servings.

CALABACITA

  2 cups cooked whole kernel corn
  3 medium zucchini squash, cut into small
    pieces
  2 green chili peppers, cut into small pieces
  1 medium onion, finely chopped
  2 cloves garlic, minced
  2 tablespoons butter or margarine
    Salt and pepper to taste
1/2 cup shredded Cheddar cheese

Combine corn, zucchini, peppers, onion, and garlic; cook until zucchini is tender. Drain and add butter, salt, and pepper. Spoon into a greased 1-quart casserole dish. Top with cheese and bake at 350° for about 10 minutes, or until cheese is melted. Yield: 6 servings.

CHINESE VEGETABLE CASSEROLE

    1 (15-ounce) can asparagus, drained
    1 (16-ounce) can tiny peas, drained
    1 (16-ounce) can Chinese vegetables,
      drained
    1 (16-ounce) can bean sprouts, drained
    1 (2-ounce) jar pimiento, chopped
    1 (3-ounce) can French fried onions
    1 cup nuts, chopped
    2 hard-cooked eggs, chopped
    1 (10-3/4-ounce) can cream of
      mushroom soup
1/2 cup butter or margarine, melted
      Salt and pepper to taste
    1 cup breadcrumbs
    1 cup shredded Cheddar cheese

Combine all vegetables, nuts, eggs, and mushroom soup. Place in a greased casserole dish. Pour butter over mixture; add salt and pepper. Top with breadcrumbs and cheese. Bake at 350° for 30 minutes. Yield: 8 to 10 servings.

MIXED VEGETABLE CASSEROLE

  2 (10-ounce) packages frozen mixed
    vegetables
  1 (10-ounce) can asparagus spears
  4 hard-cooked eggs
  1 cup mayonnaise
  1 small onion, chopped
  1 teaspoon dry mustard
  1 teaspoon Worcestershire sauce
1/2 to 1 teaspoon hot pepper sauce

Cook frozen mixed vegetables according to package directions. Cut asparagus spears into small pieces; cook over medium heat until thoroughly heated. Separate cooked egg whites and yolks. Chop cooked egg whites and combine with mayonnaise, onion, mustard, Worcestershire sauce, and hot pepper sauce; blend sauce well and combine with drained vegetables. Put into a greased, flat 2-quart casserole dish and heat at 350° until mixture begins to bubble. Garnish with crumbled egg yolks and serve hot. Yield: 8 servings.

SUMMERTIME GARDEN VEGETABLE CASSEROLE

1/2 cup butter or margarine
  1 cup sliced onions
  1 clove garlic, minced
  2 yellow squash, cut into 1/2-inch pieces
  1 medium eggplant, peeled and cut into
    1/2-inch pieces
1/2 cup all-purpose flour
  2 green peppers, chopped
  2 tomatoes, cut into wedges
  1 teaspoon salt
1/4 teaspoon oregano
1/8 teaspoon celery salt
1/8 teaspoon pepper

Melt butter in a large skillet; sauté onion and garlic until tender. Dredge squash and eggplant in flour to coat lightly. Add squash, eggplant, and green peppers to onions. Cover and simmer for 30 minutes. Add tomatoes, salt, oregano, celery salt, and pepper. Simmer an additional 20 minutes. Yield: 6 to 8 servings.

ONION SOUFFLE

6 medium onions
1 tablespoon melted butter or margarine
1 tablespoon all-purpose flour
1 cup milk
3 egg yolks, beaten
Salt and pepper
Paprika

Peel and slice onions; cook in boiling salted water over low heat until very soft. Allow to drain in a sieve for 5 minutes while making the white sauce.

Combine the melted butter and flour; stir until smooth. Add milk and cook, stirring constantly, until mixture thickens slightly. Stir in beaten egg yolks.

Chop onions very fine and season with salt and pepper. Spoon into a buttered 1-1/2-quart casserole dish; cover with white sauce and sprinkle paprika over the top. Cover and bake at 350° for 25 to 30 minutes. Yield: 6 servings.

ONIONS AU GRATIN

2 cups cooked, small, white onions
1 (10-3/4-ounce) can cream of mushroom soup
1/2 cup shredded American cheese
1/2 cup buttered breadcrumbs

Place cooked and drained onions in a greased 1-1/2-quart casserole dish. Blend mushroom soup with cheese; pour over onions. Top with buttered breadcrumbs. Bake at 325° for 20 minutes, or until sauce is bubbling. Yield: 4 to 6 servings.

SWEET-SOUR ONIONS

4 large onions, peeled
1/4 cup cider vinegar
1/4 cup melted butter or margarine
1/4 cup boiling water
1/4 cup sugar

Slice onions and arrange in a greased 1-quart baking dish. Combine remaining ingredients and pour over onions. Bake at 300° for 1 hour. Yield: 4 to 6 servings.

SCALLOPED GREEN PEAS AND ONIONS

1/4 cup butter
1/4 cup all-purpose flour
1 teaspoon salt
1 teaspoon seasoned salt
1/4 teaspoon pepper
2 cups milk
1 (10-ounce) package frozen peas, partially defrosted and broken apart
1 pound small, white onions (1- to 1-1/4 inch), peeled, or 2 (8-ounce) cans onions, drained
2 medium potatoes, peeled and thinly sliced
1 cup shredded Swiss cheese

Melt butter in a saucepan over low heat; blend in flour, salts, and pepper. Add milk, stirring constantly. Cook and stir until sauce is smooth and thick.

Arrange half of the peas, onions, and potatoes in a buttered 1-1/2-quart shallow casserole dish. Spoon half of the sauce over vegetables; sprinkle half of the cheese over the sauce. Repeat. Cover casserole dish and bake at 375° until vegetables are tender, about 1 hour. Yield: 6 servings.

MASHED POTATO CASSEROLE

8 to 10 medium boiling potatoes
Salt and pepper to taste
1 (8-ounce) package cream cheese, softened
2 eggs, lightly beaten
2 tablespoons all-purpose flour
2 tablespoons minced fresh parsley
2 tablespoons minced chives, or 1 small onion, grated
1 (3-1/2-ounce) can French fried onions

Peel and boil potatoes until tender; drain and put in a large bowl. Beat until smooth; add salt and pepper, then cream cheese, and beat again. Blend in eggs, flour, parsley, and chives, and beat thoroughly. Taste and correct seasonings if necessary; turn into a buttered casserole dish. Spread slightly crushed onions over top and bake, uncovered, at 325° for about 30 minutes, or until puffy and golden. Casserole may be prepared in the morning and refrigerated until baking time, the onions added just before placing in oven. Yield: 8 servings.

POTATO CASSEROLE SUPREME

  9 medium baking potatoes
1/2 cup butter or margarine
1-1/2 teaspoons salt
1/4 teaspoon pepper
2/3 cup warm milk
1-1/2 cups shredded Cheddar cheese
  1 cup heavy cream, whipped

Peel potatoes and boil until tender; drain and beat in large bowl of electric mixer until fluffy, adding butter, seasonings, and milk. Taste and correct seasonings if necessary; turn into a buttered shallow casserole dish. Fold cheese into whipped cream and spread over potatoes. Bake at 350° for about 25 minutes, only until golden brown. Casserole may be prepared ahead of time, the topping added just before baking. Yield: 10 servings.

POTATO PUFF CASSEROLE

  1 (8-ounce) package cream cheese, softened
  5 cups hot mashed potatoes
  1 egg, beaten
1/2 teaspoon salt
    Dash white pepper
    Dash cayenne pepper
1/2 teaspoon paprika
  2 tablespoons minced chives, or 1/2 teaspoon dehydrated onion flakes
    Melted butter or margarine

Combine softened cheese and hot potatoes, mixing until well blended. Add remaining ingredients except melted butter; beat thoroughly and turn into a buttered 1-1/2-quart casserole dish. Brush top with melted butter and bake, uncovered, at 350° for 40 minutes. This potato dish is excellent served with any beef entrée. Yield: 6 servings.

POTATO-TURNIP CASSEROLE

  2 cups quartered potatoes
  2 cups quartered turnip roots
  1 teaspoon salt
1/2 teaspoon pepper
  4 tablespoons butter or margarine
1/2 cup shredded Cheddar cheese

Cook potatoes and turnips in boiling salted water until tender. Remove from heat and drain; combine and mash. Add salt, pepper, and butter; mix well. Spoon mixture into a greased 1-quart casserole dish. Top with shredded cheese and bake at 300° for about 20 minutes, or until cheese is melted. Yield: 4 to 6 servings.

POTATOES DELUXE

  1 (8-ounce) carton commercial sour cream
3/4 cup milk
  1 (1-1/4-ounce) package sour cream sauce mix
  3 cups boiled, diced potatoes
    Salt and pepper to taste
1/2 cup buttered breadcrumbs
1/4 cup grated Parmesan cheese

Heat (do not boil) sour cream; combine milk and sour cream sauce mix, and blend well with sour cream. Layer diced potatoes and sour cream mixture in a greased 1-1/2-quart casserole dish; repeat layers. Sprinkle with salt and pepper, cover with buttered breadcrumbs, and top with Parmesan cheese. Bake at 350° for 30 minutes, or until crumbs are brown and casserole is bubbly. Yield: 8 servings.

RUTABAGA PUDDING

  2 cups mashed, cooked rutabaga, or turnips (about 1-1/4-pounds)
  2 tablespoons butter or margarine
  1 cup soft breadcrumbs
1/4 teaspoon ground mace
1/8 teaspoon pepper
  1 teaspoon salt
  1 tablespoon sugar
1/8 teaspoon ground ginger
1/2 cup milk
  1 egg, beaten
  1 tablespoon melted butter or margarine

Combine mashed rutabagas, butter, breadcrumbs, mace, pepper, salt, sugar, ginger, and milk. Add beaten egg, and spoon into a buttered 1-quart casserole dish; brush top with melted butter. Bake at 350° for 45 minutes, or until browned. Yield: 6 servings.

SCALLOPED RUTABAGA AND APPLE CASSEROLE

        1 large rutabaga, peeled and diced
        1 tablespoon butter or margarine
    1-1/2 cups peeled, sliced apples
      1/4 cup brown sugar
          Pinch ground cinnamon
      1/3 cup all-purpose flour
      1/3 cup brown sugar
        2 tablespoons butter or margarine, softened

Cook rutabaga in a small amount of boiling salted water until tender. Drain and mash; add 1 tablespoon butter. Toss sliced apples with 1/4 cup brown sugar and cinnamon. Arrange alternate layers of mashed rutabaga and sliced apples in a greased 2-quart casserole dish, beginning and ending with rutabaga. Combine flour, 1/3 cup brown sugar, and 2 tablespoons butter. Mix until crumbly and sprinkle over top of casserole. Bake at 350° for 1 hour. Yield: 6 to 8 servings.

EXOTIC SPINACH DISH

        2 (10-ounce) packages frozen spinach
        3 cups commercial sour cream
        1 (1-3/4-ounce) package dry onion
          soup mix
        2 tablespoons sherry
          Breadcrumbs (optional)

Cook spinach in unsalted water according to package directions. Drain and finely chop. Add sour cream, onion soup, and sherry. Breadcrumbs may be sprinkled over top. Place in a greased 1-1/2-quart casserole dish, and bake at 325° for 15 to 20 minutes. Yield: 8 to 10 servings.

SPINACH MADELEINE

        2 (10-ounce) packages frozen chopped
          spinach
        2 tablespoons chopped onion
        4 tablespoons butter or margarine, melted
        2 tablespoons all-purpose flour
      1/2 cup vegetable liquor
      1/2 cup evaporated milk
      1/2 teaspoon pepper
      3/4 teaspoon garlic salt
      3/4 teaspoon salt
        1 teaspoon Worcestershire sauce
        1 (6-ounce) roll of Jalapeño cheese, cut into
          small pieces
          Buttered breadcrumbs (optional)

Cook spinach according to package directions; drain and reserve liquor. Sauté onion in butter until tender. Add flour, stirring until blended and smooth. Slowly add liquor and milk, stirring constantly; cook until smooth and thick. Add pepper, garlic salt, salt, Worcestershire sauce, and cheese; stir until cheese is melted. Combine with spinach. Place in a greased 2-quart casserole dish; top with breadcrumbs. Bake at 350° for about 30 minutes, or until bubbly. Yield: 8 servings.

BAKED SPINACH WITH BACON

        3 cups cooked, drained spinach
        2 cups drained, canned tomatoes
        1 medium onion, chopped
      1/4 cup chili sauce
        1 cup cracker crumbs
        1 teaspoon salt
      1/4 teaspoon paprika
      1/2 pound American cheese, thinly sliced
        6 slices bacon

In a buttered 2-quart baking dish, alternate layers of spinach, tomatoes, onion, chili sauce, crumbs, salt, paprika, and cheese. Repeat until all the ingredients are used, ending with cheese. Sprinkle more crumbs on top. Arrange slices of bacon over top of the dish and bake at 350° for 25 minutes, or until cheese melts and bacon is crisp. Serve hot. Yield: 6 servings.

BUTTERNUT BAKE

        6 pounds butternut squash
        3 tablespoons butter or margarine
        1 tablespoon brown sugar
      1/4 teaspoon salt
        2 tablespoons raisins
        2 tablespoons chopped pecans
        1 tablespoon butter or margarine
        3 tablespoons brown sugar
      1/4 cup molasses

Cut squash in halves and remove seeds; bake, cut side down, at 400° for 50 to 60 minutes, or until tender. Scoop out pulp. Add 3 tablespoons butter, 1 tablespoon brown sugar, and salt; beat. Stir in raisins and chopped pecans; fill squash shells. Put squash in a greased 1-quart casserole dish. Combine butter, brown sugar, and molasses; drizzle over squash. Bake at 350° for 25 minutes, or until top is crusty. Yield: 6 to 8 servings.

FAVORITE SQUASH CASSEROLE

2 cups cooked squash
6 tablespoons butter or margarine
2 eggs, slightly beaten
1 teaspoon salt
1/2 teaspoon pepper
1 cup chopped onion
1 cup shredded cheese
1 cup evaporated milk
2 cups cracker crumbs

Mash cooked squash. Add other ingredients and mix well. Pour into a greased 1-quart casserole dish and bake at 375° for about 40 minutes. Yield: 6 servings.

PEANUTTY SQUASH SUPREME

2 pounds boiled squash (two 1-pound cans may be used)
1 (2-ounce) jar chopped pimientos
2 tablespoons grated onion
2 carrots, grated
1 (10-3/4-ounce) can cream of chicken soup
1 cup commercial sour cream
1 (8-ounce) package herb-seasoned stuffing mix
1 cup chopped roasted peanuts
1/2 cup butter or margarine, melted

Combine squash, pimiento, onion, and carrots. Blend soup and sour cream; stir into vegetable mixture. Toss stuffing, chopped peanuts, and butter together. Pour half the stuffing in a greased shallow 3-quart baking dish. Pour vegetable and sour cream mixture over stuffing. Top with remaining stuffing. Bake at 375° for 30 minutes. Yield: 8 to 10 servings.

SAVORY SQUASH

1-1/2 pounds yellow squash
1 small onion, minced
1 tablespoon minced parsley
1 egg, slightly beaten
1/4 cup milk
1/2 cup cottage cheese, sieved
1/2 teaspoon salt
1/2 teaspoon pepper
1 teaspoon sugar
1/4 cup finely chopped pecans

Parboil squash; mash and add all other ingredients except nuts. Place in a greased 1-quart casserole dish and sprinkle pecans over the top. Bake at 350° for about 30 to 45 minutes, or until top is browned. Yield: 6 to 8 servings.

SCALLOPED SQUASH

8 medium summer squash
1 large onion, sliced
Boiling salted water
1 egg, slightly beaten
1/2 teaspoon pepper
1/2 cup milk
2 tablespoons melted butter or margarine
1 teaspoon salt
1 cup fresh breadcrumbs
2 cups shredded sharp Cheddar cheese, divided

Wash squash and cut into 2-inch pieces. Cook squash and onion in boiling salted water for about 10 minutes, or until squash is tender; drain. Arrange squash in a greased 2-1/2-quart casserole dish. Combine egg, pepper, milk, butter, salt, breadcrumbs, and 1 cup cheese; mix well and pour over squash. Sprinkle top with remaining cup of cheese. Bake at 350° for 30 minutes. Yield: 8 servings.

SQUASH-CHEESE CASSEROLE

3 pounds small yellow squash
1 small green pepper, minced
1/4 cup minced onion
4 tablespoons butter or margarine
2 teaspoons sugar (optional)
1 cup milk
4 slices dry toasted bread
1-1/2 cups shredded sharp Cheddar cheese, divided
3 eggs, beaten
Few drops hot pepper sauce

Slice squash; combine with green pepper and onion in boiling salted water. Cook until squash is tender. Remove from heat and drain. Add butter and sugar; stir until melted.

Combine milk, crumbled toasted bread, 1 cup cheese, eggs, and hot pepper sauce. Add to squash mixture and mix well. Divide mixture evenly between two greased 2-quart casserole dishes or put all in a 4-quart casserole dish. Sprinkle 1/2 cup shredded cheese over the top, cover, and bake at 350° for about 20 minutes. Yield: 10 servings.

SQUASH AND CARROT CASSEROLE

8 yellow squash, cooked and drained
6 carrots, cooked and drained
2 eggs
3 tablespoons chopped onion
1/4 cup butter or margarine
2 tablespoons all-purpose flour

Beat the cooked squash and carrots together. Then beat in all other ingredients. Turn into a greased shallow casserole dish. Bake at 350° for 1 hour. This can be prepared in the morning and refrigerated until time to bake. Yield: 4 to 5 servings.

SQUASH AND CHEESE CASSEROLE

    4 pounds yellow squash
    2 pounds zucchini squash
    1 large onion, chopped
    2 tablespoons sugar
    1 teaspoon salt
    2 cups water
    1 cup shredded Cheddar cheese
    1 cup shredded American cheese
  1/2 cup butter or margarine
    1 cup half-and-half

Slice squash; peel and chop onion. Place in a saucepan. Add sugar, salt, and water; simmer until squash is tender, about 20 minutes. Drain and mash. In a buttered 2-quart casserole dish, alternate layers of squash and mixed cheeses. Dot with butter. Pour half-and-half over the top and bake at 300° for 15 minutes. Yield: 8 servings.

SQUASH DELIGHT

    1 pound squash
    1 large onion, grated
    1 cup shredded Cheddar cheese
  1/4 cup cream
    2 tablespoons butter or margarine
    1 egg, beaten
      Dash ground nutmeg
      Salt and pepper to taste
  1/2 cup cracker crumbs
      Paprika

Cook squash and onion in a small amount of salted water; drain. Add cheese, cream, butter,

egg, nutmeg, salt, and pepper. Mix well. Pour into a buttered casserole dish. Top with cracker crumbs and paprika. Bake at 350° until mixture bubbles and crumbs are brown, about 25 minutes. Yield: 4 to 6 servings.

SQUASH-SWISS CHEESE CASSEROLE

    3 to 4 pounds yellow squash
    2 medium onions, minced
    2 bay leaves
      About 6 sprigs parsley
  1/2 teaspoon leaf thyme
    6 tablespoons butter or margarine
    6 tablespoons all-purpose flour
    3 cups milk
      Dash salt
    1 teaspoon seasoned salt
      Several dashes ground nutmeg
      Dash Worcestershire sauce
    4 egg yolks, beaten
      About 1-1/3 cups shredded Swiss cheese, divided
      Cayenne pepper
      Buttered breadcrumbs

Cut squash into 1/3-inch slices. Place in a large saucepan with onion, bay leaves, parsley, and thyme. Cover with boiling salted water and cook until squash is barely tender. Drain, remove parsley and bay leaves, and set aside.

In a saucepan, heat butter; blend in flour; then gradually add milk and salt. Cook, stirring constantly, until thickened. To the sauce, add seasoned salt, nutmeg, and Worcestershire sauce. Remove from heat; gradually blend in egg yolks (by adding small amount of the hot sauce to yolks beaten in a small bowl, then adding a little more, etc., then returning all back to the saucepan). Stir in 1 cup cheese and add cayenne pepper.

Combine squash with sauce, stirring gently; turn into a large buttered baking dish about 2 inches deep. Mix remaining cheese with an equal amount (or more, if needed) of buttered breadcrumbs. Sprinkle over squash and bake at 350° for about 35 minutes, or until top is bubbly and brown. Leftovers freeze well. Yield: 12 servings.

Allspice

Allspice is a delicately fragrant spice which tastes like a blend of nutmeg, cinnamon, and cloves. Allspice is appetizing in fruit dishes, vegetables (especially carrots and eggplant), and meat sauces.

SUMMER SQUASH CASSEROLE

    4 medium yellow squash
1/3 cup butter or margarine
1/3 cup chopped onion
    2 hard-cooked eggs, chopped
1/2 cup cubed Cheddar cheese
    1 cup corn chips

Boil squash until almost done. Melt butter in
skillet; add onion and sauté until tender. Add
squash; mix well and spoon into a greased
1-quart casserole dish. Add eggs and cheese;
sprinkle with corn chips. Bake at 350° for 10
to 15 minutes, or just until cheese is melted.
Serve at once. Yield: 4 servings.

CHEESY ZUCCHINI CASSEROLE

    4 to 6 tender zucchini squash
    2 hard-cooked eggs, sliced
    2 tablespoons butter or margarine
    2 tablespoons all-purpose flour
1/4 teaspoon salt
    1 cup milk
1/2 cup shredded Cheddar cheese
       Cayenne pepper to taste
    4 to 6 tablespoons buttered breadcrumbs
1/4 cup grated Parmesan or Romano cheese

Wash squash well; split each lengthwise into
3 pieces; boil in salted water for 5 minutes.
Drain well and place in a greased shallow baking
dish; place sliced eggs over squash. Melt butter
over low heat; stir in flour and salt until well
blended. Add milk and cook, stirring constantly,
until mixture thickens. Add shredded Cheddar
cheese and stir until cheese is melted. Pour over
squash and eggs. Taste and add more salt if
necessary. Add cayenne pepper. Top with
buttered breadcrumbs and sprinkle grated
Parmesan cheese over the top. Bake at 375° for
25 to 30 minutes, or until mixture is bubbly and
brown. Yield: 6 to 8 servings.

DELICIOUS ZUCCHINI

    8 small zucchini squash, sliced lengthwise
    2 tomatoes, cut into eighths
1/2 green pepper, cut into thin strips
3/4 cup chopped onion
1/2 teaspoon salt
1/2 teaspoon Beau Monde seasoning
1/4 teaspoon pepper
1/4 cup grated Parmesan cheese
1/2 teaspoon sugar
1/4 cup butter or margarine, melted

Place zucchini slices in a buttered, oblong
casserole dish. Place tomatoes, green pepper, and
onion between zucchini slices. Sprinkle salt,
Beau Monde seasoning, pepper, cheese, and
sugar on top. Drizzle butter evenly over the top.
Bake, uncovered, at 350° for 45 minutes to 1
hour. Yield: 6 servings.

ZUCCHINI AND CORN CASSEROLE

    6 medium zucchini squash, sliced
1/2 cup diced onion
    2 tablespoons butter or margarine, melted
    1 cup cooked cream-style corn
       Dash ground cumin
       Dash garlic salt
1/4 teaspoon pepper
3/4 teaspoon salt
       Dash paprika
1/4 cup seasoned croutons
1/2 cup shredded Cheddar cheese

Sauté squash and onion in melted butter until
tender, stirring constantly. Stir in corn, cumin,
garlic salt, pepper, salt, and paprika. Mix well
and spoon mixture into a greased 1-1/2-quart
casserole dish. Sprinkle top with seasoned
croutons and sprinkle shredded cheese on top.
Bake at 300° for 30 minutes. Yield: 6 to 8
servings.

ZUCCHINI-CHEESE BAKE

    3 medium zucchini squash
    1 (4-3/4-ounce) can chicken spread
    1 (11-ounce) can Cheddar cheese soup
1/4 cup milk
1/2 teaspoon dry mustard
1/2 cup combination grain cereal flakes

Trim zucchini and cut each in half lengthwise.
Parboil for 10 minutes in salted water. Drain
and arrange in a greased shallow 2-quart baking
dish. Spread top of each zucchini half with
chicken spread, dividing evenly. Mix soup, milk,
and mustard. Pour mixture over zucchini and
sprinkle with cereal. Bake at 350° for 30
minutes, or until tender. Yield: 6 servings.

BRANDIED SWEET POTATOES

1 tablespoon freshly grated orange peel
3 to 4 oranges, peeled
1/4 cup firmly packed brown sugar
1/2 cup brandy
1/4 cup half-and-half
1/4 cup melted butter or margarine
1 teaspoon salt
4 cups mashed, cooked sweet potatoes

Grate peel from orange. Slice 1 peeled orange into cartwheels; set aside. Cut remaining oranges into very small pieces to yield 2 cups drained fruit. Sprinkle orange pieces with brown sugar; set aside. Heat orange peel, brandy, half-and-half, butter, and salt together. Beat mixture into mashed sweet potatoes until well blended. Stir in drained, sweetened orange pieces. Spoon mixture into a well-greased 1-1/2-quart casserole dish; top with orange slices. Sprinkle lightly with additional brown sugar, if desired. Bake, uncovered, at 350° for 35 to 40 minutes. Casserole may be made in advance and refrigerated until ready to bake. Yield: 8 servings.

FAVORITE SWEET POTATOES

1/2 cup brown sugar, divided
2/3 cup orange juice, divided
1/3 cup butter or margarine, melted and divided
2 (1-pound) cans sweet potatoes, drained
2 eggs
1 teaspoon salt
1/4 teaspoon cloves
1 teaspoon ground cinnamon
1 cup chopped pecans

Combine 1/4 cup brown sugar, 2 teaspoons orange juice, and 2 teaspoons butter; mix and set aside to use for glaze topping. Whip potatoes until smooth; beat in eggs. Add remaining brown sugar, orange juice, and butter. Add salt, cloves, and cinnamon; mix well and pour into a 1-1/2-quart casserole dish. Sprinkle pecans on top. Pour glaze topping over pecans. Bake at 350° for 40 minutes. Yield: 6 servings.

GLAZED SWEET POTATO CASSEROLE

1 cup light corn syrup
1/4 cup butter or margarine
1/3 cup pineapple juice
8 to 10 canned or cooked sweet potatoes, halved
1/4 cup pineapple tidbits, drained
1/3 cup pecan halves

Combine corn syrup, butter, and pineapple juice in a saucepan. Place over medium heat and simmer for 5 minutes. Place potatoes in a greased 13- x 9- x 2-inch baking dish. Sprinkle with pineapple tidbits and pecans. Add syrup mixture. Bake at 375° for 40 minutes. Baste every 10 minutes with syrup mixture. Serve hot. Yield: 6 to 8 servings.

ORANGE CANDIED SWEET POTATOES

4 medium sweet potatoes, unpeeled
1/3 cup brown sugar, firmly packed
1/3 cup sugar
3/4 cup orange juice
Dash salt
1/4 cup butter or margarine

Cook potatoes in boiling salted water until barely soft. Remove from water and cool. Remove skin and cut into quarters or 3/4-inch slices. Place in a greased flat 1-1/2-quart baking dish. Combine other ingredients in a small saucepan and bring to a boil; pour over potatoes in the baking dish. Cover dish and bake at 375° for 25 minutes; uncover and bake an additonal 15 to 20 minutes, or until syrup has cooked down and potatoes are glazed. Yield: 8 servings.

SWEET POTATO-APPLE CASSEROLE

4 medium sweet potatoes
4 medium apples
1/2 cup sugar
1 cup water
Butter or margarine
1/2 cup brown sugar
Breadcrumbs

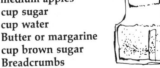

Wash sweet potatoes thoroughly and boil until tender. Meanwhile, pare, core, and slice the apples and place in a saucepan with sugar and water. Boil slowly until the potatoes are tender. Peel potatoes and cut lengthwise into slices. Place a layer of sliced potatoes in a greased 1-quart casserole dish. Dot with butter and sprinkle with brown sugar. Add a layer of apples. Repeat layers until all ingredients are used. Add liquid from apples. Sprinkle with breadcrumbs and add a few dots of butter. Bake at 400° for 15 minutes. Yield: 6 servings.

Paprika

Paprika, the cool and mild member of the pepper family, highlights lightly flavored foods such as eggs, poultry, seafood, and sauces. Its slightly sweet flavor and brilliant red color make this spice a favorite garnish.

PRALINE YAM CASSEROLE WITH ORANGE SAUCE

 4 medium yams, cooked, peeled, and quartered, or 2 (16-ounce) cans yams, drained
 2 eggs
1/2 cup firmly packed dark brown sugar, divided
1/3 cup butter or margarine, melted and divided
 1 teaspoon salt
1/2 cup pecan halves
  Orange Sauce

Mash yams in a large bowl. Beat in eggs, 1/4 cup brown sugar, 2 tablespoons melted butter, and salt. Pour into a greased 1-quart casserole dish. Arrange pecan halves in a pattern over the top; sprinkle with remaining 1/4 cup brown sugar and drizzle with remaining melted butter. Bake, uncovered, at 375° for 20 minutes. Serve with warm Orange Sauce. Yield: 6 servings.

Orange Sauce

1/3 cup sugar
 1 tablespoon cornstarch
1/8 teaspoon salt
 1 teaspoon grated orange peel
 1 cup orange juice
 1 tablespoon freshly squeezed lemon juice
 2 tablespoons butter or margarine
 1 tablespoon Grand Marnier
 3 dashes angostura bitters

Blend sugar, cornstarch, and salt in a saucepan; add grated orange peel, orange juice, and lemon juice. Bring to a boil over medium heat, stirring constantly until sauce is thickened. Remove from heat and stir in butter, Grand Marnier, and angostura bitters. Yield: 1 cup.

SWEET POTATO-APPLE-SAUERKRAUT CASSEROLE

 2 medium cooking apples, peeled and sliced
1/3 cup brown sugar
 2 cups drained sauerkraut
 3 cups cooked, mashed sweet potatoes

Place half the sliced apples in the bottom of a greased 2-quart casserole dish; sprinkle with half the brown sugar. Add half the sauerkraut, then half the mashed sweet potatoes. Repeat layers. Bake at 350° for 30 to 40 minutes. Yield: 8 servings.

SWEET POTATO CASSEROLE

 3 cups cooked, mashed sweet potatoes
1/2 cup sugar
 2 eggs, beaten
1/2 teaspoon salt
1/4 cup butter or margarine, melted
1/2 cup milk
1-1/2 teaspoon vanilla extract
1/2 cup brown sugar
1/3 cup all-purpose flour
 1 cup chopped nuts
 3 tablespoons butter or margarine, melted

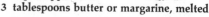

Combine potatoes, sugar, eggs, salt, 1/4 cup butter, milk, and vanilla. Spoon into a greased 1- to 1-1/2-quart baking dish. Combine brown sugar, flour, nuts, and melted butter. Spread over sweet potato mixture. Bake at 350° for 35 minutes. Yield: 8 servings.

ZESTY SCALLOPED TOMATOES

3-1/2 cups coarsely chopped, peeled fresh tomatoes
1/4 cup minced onion
 2 tablespoons minced green pepper (optional)
 1 teaspoon salt
  Dash pepper
1/2 teaspoon sugar
 2 cups soft bread cubes
 2 tablespoons butter or margarine, melted

Combine tomatoes, onion, green pepper, salt, pepper, and sugar. Place alternate layers of tomato mixture and bread cubes in a greased 2-quart casserole dish, ending with bread cubes. Drizzle melted butter over the top. Bake at 375° for 20 to 30 minutes. Yield: 6 servings.

CASSEROLE-BAKED TOMATOES

 2 (1-pound) cans solid-packed tomatoes
 2 tablespoons brown sugar
 2 teaspoons salt
1/2 teaspoon chervil
1/2 teaspoon seasoned salt
 2 small onions, minced
 2 tablespoons chopped chives
1/8 teaspoon pepper
1/2 teaspoon dillweed
  Coarse dry breadcrumbs

Place tomatoes in a casserole dish. Mix in all other ingredients except breadcrumbs. Scatter crumbs on top and bake at 250° for 2 hours. Yield: 8 to 10 servings.

Index

Index